BEYOND
THE
RHETORIC

ALSO BY WILLIAM D. GAIRDNER

Disruptive Essays: There Are No Safe Spaces in This Book! (2018)

The Great Divide: Why Liberals and Conservatives Will Never, Ever Agree (2015)

The Trouble With Canada … Still!: A Citizen Speaks Out (2011)

The Book of Absolutes: A Critique of Relativism and a Defence of Universals (2008)

Oh, Oh, Canada! A Voice from the Conservative Resistance (2008)

The Trouble with Democracy: A Citizen Speaks Out (2001)

After Liberalism: Essays in Search of Freedom, Virtue, and Order (1998)

On Higher Ground: Reclaiming a Civil Society (1996)

Constitutional Crack-Up: Canada and the Coming Showdown with Quebec (1994)

The War Against the Family: A Parent Speaks Out on the Political, Economic, and Social Policies That Threaten Us All (1992)

The Trouble with Canada: A Citizen Speaks Out (1990)

The Critical Wager: Essays on Criticism and the Architecture of Ideology (1982)

AS TRANSLATOR AND COMMENTATOR

The French Traveler: Adventure, Exploration & Indian Life in 18th-Century Canada (2019)

AS EDITOR

Canada's Founding Debates (1999) [with Janet Ajzenstat, Ian Gentles & Paul Romney]

Alphonse G. Juilland, PhD, **Rethinking Track and Field: The Future of the World's Oldest Sport** (2002)

WILLIAM
GAIRDNER

BEYOND THE RHETORIC

A COLLECTION OF IN-DEPTH ESSAYS
PUBLISHED IN THE EPOCH TIMES

EXPANDED EDITION

Original Kindle Edition published by The Epoch Times:
Copyright © 2020
Contributors:
Publisher: Stephen Gregory
Editor-in-Chief: Jasper Fakkert
Editors: Kat Piper, Channaly Philipp
Digital Managing Editor: Aloysio Carrilho dos Santos
Copy Editors: Julia Huang, Joseph Sabo, Jamey Walston, Patton Diao
Author's website: www.WilliamGairdner.ca

Cover and interior design, typesetting, online publishing, and printing
by Daniel Crack, Kinetics Design, KDbooks.ca
www.linkedin.com/in/kdbooks/

For Jean

Contents

Eleanor Roosevelt holding the poster of the Universal Declaration of Human Rights, Lake Success, New York. November 1949.

Source: FDR Presidential Library & Museum

1.   The Fallacy of Human Rights

DECEMBER 26, 2022

"**H**uman rights" are everywhere, and are everywhere described with astonishing vagueness as something "inherent" in all human beings, simply because we are human.

It's a circular assertion.

Largely in reaction to the tragedies and slaughters of World War II, the United Nations in 1948 produced a celebrated Universal Declaration of Human Rights announcing 30 rights, many of the common liberal variety that attempt to protect individuals from arbitrary power. But then, beginning with Article 22, economic, social, and cultural rights are included, which are claims to state action, rather than to freedom from state action.

Then, declared in Article 29, we find the assertion that "everyone has duties to the community," but with no mention of what those duties might be. Canada's Charter of Rights and Freedoms (1982) makes no mention of "duties," or "obligations" whatsoever, as if 35 million citizens each have a bundle of rights, but no one is obligated to fulfill them.

The Rights Boom

The idea of declaring human rights — they are always "declared" — has become an inflationary pastime. Occasional reports indicate every living human being (dead people have a lot of them, too) now has about 400 human rights, but no one knows for sure. To date, a half dozen "core" international rights treaties have been signed by more than 150 nations, many of which are quite hostile to Western secularization, support the subordination of women in religion and law, and employ lots of child labor, among other abuses.

Furthermore, many ostensibly rights-observant nations breezily carry on business with rights-abusing nations, all of which cheapens the very idea of a right.

A few rights considered normal by almost everyone throughout the ages are the right to life (though in many countries — Canada is one — you don't have this right until you are "born alive"), innocence until proven guilty (not always observed), to self-defense, to peaceful free speech, to property, to free assembly short of public disturbance or anarchy, and the like. Though often breached, these rights have had a historical pedigree in the common law of most Western nations long preceding the current rights fever.

But the bulk of new modern rights are of dubious merit, to say the least, and hundreds seem simply frivolous. Declared are the rights to travel, to food, water, health care, to have a job, to receive a living wage (but with no mention of who will be legally forced to supply such things), and — I almost forgot — "sex workers' rights." Then we have declarations of a "right to a toilet," a "right to the internet," and, by the French recently — the most amusing so far — a "right to idleness."

Many rights critics such as Eric Posner, author of "The Twilight of Human Rights Law" (2014), have concluded that human rights laws are "hopelessly ambiguous," that rights-regimes are promoting a mostly Western "progressive" (code for leftist/statist/secular) conception of how we ought to live, and that signings of human rights treaties, which are easily ignored with genocides, slavery, child labor, and extra-judicial killings, are "not so much an act of idealism as an act of hubris."

Another critic described the U.N.'s post-war Declaration as "a funeral wreath laid on the grave of wartime hopes," and conservative philosopher the late Roger Scruton went deeper: "Instead of limiting the power of the state, alleged human rights have begun to enhance that power … [in] a declaration of war on the majority culture." A serious turn.

Disturbingly, Canada has long since signed international rights treaties such as the U.N. Declaration of the Rights of the Child (1959), which do seem to express some fine-sounding rights, until it sinks in that children can't exercise rights. Their putative rights must be exercised for them, usually against their own parents by bureaucrats keen to expose families — and nations — that don't fit a liberal notion of "promoting social progress," as urged in the preamble to this declaration.

International rights treaties in fact seem intended to operate not as inter-national, but rather as supra-national powers exerting significant progressive control over the internal policies of signatory nations. And yet, there are many nations that differ profoundly on the basic question of human rights. For example, an observant Muslim — there are 2 billion Muslims on earth — will tell you, in no uncertain terms that human beings do not have rights. Only God has rights. Humans have duties. The meaning of "Islam," after all, is "submission" … to the word and law of God.

Nevertheless, Islam has published its own catalog of supposed "human rights," and at first, it looks as if they have caved to our Western rights delirium. But they haven't. Islamic human rights are each strictly qualified and limited by the law of Shariah and the Koran. Better believe it.

Further investigation shows that some declarations of abstract rights — they are all abstract — beginning with the infamous French Declaration of the Rights of Man and the Citizen (1789) that ignited the modern rights boom (as well as the Terror of the French Revolution) are quite careful to include a reminder, usually in a preamble, of the "duties" of citizens. But duties are never mentioned again. Instead, there are a dozen seldom-remarked phrases such as "determined by the law" attached to its 17 articles. In short, human rights exist — if they can be said to exist at all — only in relation to power, whether civil, legal, moral, or political.

So, what's a right?

Ignoring virtue-signaling, placard-waving, and other political gestures, I would say a "right" boils down to a defensible claim that may be negative or positive. The controlling image of the former is the solitary individual shaking a fist at power: "Get your foot off my neck." As long as you can defend such a negative claim we could say, not that you have an inherent right — like you have a heart or a kidney — but that you are exercising a customary legal power (if such exists) to be left alone; to do whatever the law/power/duty and custom permit.

The most common negative rights in the West have always been best defended not by abstract declarations and phrases, which are easily warped in meaning by judges and politicians, but by formally executed actual documents filed in countless legal cabinets, homes, offices, and legislatures across the world, such as a writ of habeas corpus, a deed to your property, a signed marriage license, a business contract, an executed will, and so on.

So-called positive rights are very different and amount to a claim to something you think you deserve or are owed, usually by some level of government, by a corporation, or by an identifiable person or entity against which you may be able to force performance of the right. Positive rights these days generally are claims to fulfillment of a contract, or to promised goods and services such as "free" medical care, a government pension, a minimum wage, and the like.

In ordinary common law, I'm said to have a property right, without which there's very little meaning to the right of personal freedom, for if you can't legally own a home, a car, a bicycle, a pair of shoes, and buy or sell such things at will, your sphere of freedom is very limited. As it happens, Canada's Charter makes no mention whatsoever of a property right. But even if it were mentioned, if you can't stop suspicious-looking strangers from wandering all over your property or barging into your home, and police refuse to evict them, your property right is useless because it isn't actionable or, as I say, defensible.

In short, there's always a connection between the idea of a right, and one or another power that may — or may not — be able to enforce your claim. If you're stranded alone on the moon, however, your claim to a "right" of any kind is immediately ludicrous because there's no entity obliged to fulfill it.

By now it looks like right equals might, and the idea of a free-floating "inherent" right as a permanent "natural" quality of a human being seems pure fantasy. Where did such a fantasy come from? The Western notion of an indwelling personal "natural right," concludes historian David Ritchie, is the logical outgrowth of the Protestant Reformation's appeal to private judgment. It appeared in all its "metaphysical nakedness" as a revolt against the authority of tradition, and continues today, mostly in Protestant countries, in the name of ... individual rights.

Strikingly, the Euro-Germanic tradition of rights-talk firmly rejects the notion of the individual "lone-rights-bearer" favored in the Anglo-American sphere. Germany's Basic Law, for example, states that "everyone has duties to the community." Article 16 devotes an entire section to "protection of family relations," and declares that citizen freedom is "limited by the moral code." But nowhere in Canadian rights declarations do we find any mention of moral codes or community limitations on liberty.

In fact, in the infamous "Swingers" case (R v. Labaye, 2006) having to do with the effort of a Quebec community to close down a neighborhood sex club operating above a local convenience store frequented by children, the high court specifically cited J.S. Mill's libertarian "Harm Principle" as a new individualist moral standard that must henceforth replace community standards. That's just one example — there are plenty more — of "a declaration of war on the majority culture."

A Little More Rights Scrutiny

But what about the logic — or rather, illogic — of human rights? It doesn't look good. The first, and still most devastating logical demolition of the entire concept of human rights was Jeremy Bentham's "Anarchical Fallacies," composed in 1815 as a frontal attack on the French Declaration of 1789. Logically, and embarrassingly for rights enthusiasts at a loss for replies even today, Bentham trashed the entire underlying theory long ago. Let us examine his attack, keying off his response to assumptions of the Declaration.

Assumption:
Men are born free and remain free and equal in rights

Bentham argues this is simply and clearly false. Worse, a lie at the heart of our civilization. Humans aren't born free, but helpless, wholly dependent, and utterly subject to parental and societal will and law. Society, he states, "is held together only by the sacrifices men can be induced to make of the gratifications they demand." Declarations of rights falsely said to exist prior to government, on the other hand, in effect counsel the ignoring of all sacrifice of the passions, implicitly authorizing insurrection against established society if imagined rights are violated.

Bentham again: "All rights are made at the expense of liberty," for "no liberty can be given to one man but in proportion as it is taken from another," as when your liberty to walk on your property is gained only by denying this liberty to others. How is your house made yours? "By debarring everyone else from the liberty of entering it without your leave." Hence, "all laws creative of liberty, are, as far as they go, abrogative of liberty." Rights advocates attempt to avoid this obvious truth by claiming rights as original absolutes that trump all laws.

Assumption:
Rights are inherent

The undeniable truth that a right is a positive or negative claim on another person or entity negates the assumption rights are inherent in each of us and self-fulfilling, for there can be no such thing as a right for one without a corresponding obligation upon another person, or entity, to satisfy the right. If you declare "I have a right to marry," for example, you are also declaring that someone else has an obligation to marry you.

Assumption:
Governments are created by free contract of the people

This idea remains a popular fiction. But history reveals that every government that has ever existed has been the evolved product of conquest, habit, custom, tradition, or some combination of the same. The underlying assertion found in theorists such as John Locke that governments exist only by contract of the people and are legitimized by consent, is historically false, as the philosopher David Hume pointed out long ago. Why? Because a pre-existing government and a prior system of established law are required in order to establish and enforce contracts in the first place.

And so, Bentham again: "Contracts came from government, not government from contracts." Contractarians (Bentham was taking aim at John Locke) seek "to excite and keep up a spirit of resistance to all laws" as if "in [them] is the perfection of virtue and wisdom," but in all others, "the extremity of wickedness and folly. Our will shall consequently reign," they insist, "without control, and forever: reign now we are living — reign after we are dead."

This extreme focus on individual will found an immediate home in French revolutionary law, which declared that if either party (not both, but either) to a contract withdraws consent, the contract is ended. The longstanding contractual standard of "Two to make it, two to break it," overnight became "Two to make it, one to break it." Just so, in attempting to freeze political reality in a written rights contract, in a kind of "hubris of the now," contractarians seek to imprison all future generations in the will of the present, thereby robbing them of their freedom to change … the contract.

Assumption:
Human rights are natural

The declaration of human rights as natural, inalienable, and made … by the goddess "Nature," prior to, and excluding all government, is again, Bentham insists, repugnant to all laws and a recipe for perpetual revolution. The very word "natural" stands in opposition to "legal." That's why Bentham described the entire notion of rights prior to law as "terrorist language … the maxim of the anarchist," and then, in one of Western history's most memorable lines, as "nonsense upon stilts." For merely "wishing there were such things as rights, are not rights," just as "hunger is not bread." As to limitations? Checkmate again, for "what is every man's right, is no man's right."

Assumption:
The right of resistance to oppression

Bentham: "In proportion as a law of any kind … is unpleasant to a man … he, of course, looks upon it as oppression," and so, all rights enthusiasts insist, you should "submit not to any decree or other act of power, of the justice of which you are not yourself perfectly convinced." By now, Bentham is rollicking, arguing that rights claims tend to reduce to a demand for the satisfaction of personal will. Rights claimants are little Napoleons. And so, "if a constable call upon you to serve in the militia, shoot the constable and not the enemy; if the commander of a press-gang trouble you, push him into the sea; if a bailiff, throw him out the window. If a judge sentences you to be imprisoned or put to death, have a dagger ready, and take a stroke first at the judge."

Some Conclusions

The fundamental assertion of all rights documents is that listed rights such as we find in the prototypical French Declaration (and in the Canadian Charter) are "imprescriptible" — meaning inalienable, universal, true forever, equal for all, cannot be altered, and so on. As applied in pre-democratic societies where absolute sovereignty lies with rulers, declarations of practical (as distinct from abstract) rights — as found in "Magna Carta" (1215) — may be an effective popular shield against abuse from above. But in democracies, where sovereignty is considered to reside in the popular will itself, rights, once declared inalienable, become an unchangeable shield against new expressions of a better will by the people themselves. The people then exist in a rights trap.

So the final, and ironic, stage of Western rights hysteria — the death throes, so to speak — seems to be when progressive elites and judges attempting to continue the re-engineering of public policy must (as in Canada) resort to inventing and legitimizing phantom interpretations of various declared rights, thus undermining public confidence in the value of a document that says nothing about them.•

Mussolini leading the "passo romano", a military step introduced from the nazi goose step, January, 27 1938. This picture was censored by Mussolini.

Source: M. Franzinelli, E. V. Marino, Il Duce proibito, Mondadori, 2005, p. 64

2. The Rise of Microfascism in Western Democracies

THERE has never been much agreement on the definition of fascism. Nevertheless, the impression that, whatever its form, it always has to do with the triumph of the will over nature, seems a penetrating truth about early fascism as well as its more recent manifestations. The French saying *Chassez le naturel, il revient au galop* ("banish the natural, and it comes galloping back") is a truth of nature that, absent the help of massively oppressive state powers, no degree of will could ever succeed in altering for long. Despite this bald reality, the recent history of the West has been a disturbing and repetitive narrative centered on the complexities and catastrophes that result from efforts to banish nature.

In what follows, I argue that all the modern, unnatural, and therefore anti-human, attempts to bend nature and human nature to the will have been expressed in two basic forms, one macro, the other micro. By the end, we may want to ask to what peculiar quirk of nature we owe our apparently insatiable hunger to banish it.

Before looking at the differences between these two forms, however, let us ask about the origin of the word "fascism," for which it suffices to recall the imperial image of victorious Roman legions marching in triumph with the *fasces* — bundles of bound sticks from the center of which protruded a menacing axe — borne aloft. The symbolism could not be clearer: Roman power binds and controls all individuals as one. This form of macrofascism, originally an engine of military empire, eventually found its most coherent modern political and moral expression in the "Social Contract" (1762) of Jean-Jacques Rousseau, in which he insisted on the complete absorption of all individual wills into a single national, or General Will. The plainest description of this template for what we now recognize as a uniquely European form of totalitarian democracy may be glimpsed in his novel "Émile" *(1762)*, where we read of his ambition to "transport the I into the common unity, with the result that each individual believes himself no longer one, but a part of the unity, and no longer feels except within the whole." This was the first fully articulated political formula for what may be called a democracy of the one, rather than of the many. It served as a guide and moral justification for the murderous fanaticism of the Jacobins during the French Revolution, and then for Hitler's Nazi party as well as Mussolini's Italian Fascists. Hitler often burbled publicly, "This revolution of ours is the exact counterpart of the French Revolution," and Mussolini famously formalized his own philosophy in the slogan *democrazia organizatta!*

These recent forms of macrofascism, whether French, Italian, German, or Russian, have always been collectivist, secular, and militant, striving through the fearsome top-down powers of the State to draw all things into the ambit of a single pattern of national — or in the case of communism, international — will, always expressed by the subjugation and assimilation by force of things spontaneous, private, and natural to artificial and unnatural public designs. For private religious belief? A secular and wholly materialist belief. For concepts of transcendent natural law? Man-made laws only. For the private family? An array of public programs and services from national daycare, to health care, to subsidized housing, to old-age homes. For private enterprise and free markets? Intensive regulation, ever-higher taxation, and the direction of the forces of production to state ends. For countless voluntary community organizations? Equivalent public organizations. In short, it is a will that leads to the Nanny State, cradle to grave.

The German word that described this transformation of the private and natural into the public and artificial was *gleichschaltung*, which means "to bring everything into line." Take note of the word "line," for the variety of methods used to force all things natural, spontaneous, curved, and organic (think of all those charming European village laneways, a map of which looks like a biological or botanical growth) into geometrically rigid lines and grids, conceptual or actual, is truly astonishing. The monomaniacally linear architect Le Corbusier, gloating upon his fantasies for the perfect Soviet city, could not resist sniffing that "curved lines constitute paralysis, and the winding path is the path of donkeys."

On this general theme of regulation, however, our liberal-democratic regimes cannot afford to be smug. Although we have never had to pack machine guns to enforce our softer, but no less pervasive, brand of statism, most of the policy specifics common to macrofascism are recognizable in our own "progressive" regimes. To wit, more than three-quarters of the German and Italian programs (and a lot of the communist ones) are virtually indistinguishable from our own political fare, and this is true for all the Great Society, New Society, or Just Society programs of our modern "liberal" States. No matter which democracy we look at, we find ever-increasing statism, taxation, debt, and regulation. Everywhere, the larger national or federal political units continue to absorb and subjugate — bring into line — the smaller states, provinces, regions, and municipalities; so everywhere, we see more "democracy," but less freedom. And what might be the reason?

Some say that all fascism is a reactionary response to a perceived loss of natural community. But its deeper sources are more likely rooted in despair over the glaring imperfections of human existence, most notably our anger at the apparent absence of justice on Earth (which is to say, at our perceived abandonment by God). From this dejection has sprung the modern resolve to go it alone, so to speak: if there is no God to make earthly existence perfect, then we'll do it by our own means, powered by the belief that human beings (at least of the planning type) are actually godlets ("made in the image of God" is the template) who have an obligation to impose a uniform design of perfection on all natural but imperfect expressions of human life. Secularization began in earnest with the rise of the modern State during the French Revolution, Rousseau's "Contract" in hand. Its effects then and since may be seen in sobering detail in James C. Scott's "Seeing Like a State" (Yale, 1998), which traces various militant efforts to create "a single national society perfectly legible from the center," in which all things natural and non-conforming were to be "denaturalized" (a cure that operates more like a disease).

The standard recipe for spreading this disease requires only a few ingredients to create a "full-fledged disaster." The first is a comprehensive aspiration to the "refashioning of social habits and of human nature itself." The second is an ideology legitimizing the "unrestrained use of the power of the modern state" for the satisfaction of human needs according to a "rational" model. The third is "a weakened or prostrate civil society that lacks the capacity to resist these plans." In a putatively democratic age ruled by a supposed "sovereignty of the people," this abasement of civil society is surely the saddest element.

From this ideological gestation, the modern Statist dystopia, which relies on well-worn tools of regimentation, has emerged. Examples are the imposition of official languages by means of which whole regions formerly illegible to central government may be linguistically subdued and culturally incorporated. Another standard tool is the eradication of all local systems of weights and measures. The foot? The pound? The ounce? Such intimately natural human measures have been made illegal in most nations by metrication, the most zealous proponents of which always argue that a more "rational" unit will produce a more rational (and, therefore, a more easily organized) citizenry. The most menacing novelties of modern statism are surely the highly precise and all-pervasive instruments of statecraft, such as computerized data, encrypted identity cards, statistical bureaus, modes of instant satellite communication, precise cadastral (tax) maps, intensive tax-harvesting (by installment) on an unprecedented scale, pervasive State invasions of the private realm, sophisticated spying and security measures, and much more. None of these modern tools now common to our putatively free nations could have been imagined for a moment in even the most frenzied dreams of any absolutist king or despot in all prior human history. It is indisputable that we were much freer (less regulated, spied upon, and taxed) before the onset of modern democracy.

Personal examples of the loss of freedom to the macrofascist will over nature are very close to many of us. One of the purposes of modern property codification and taxation regimes has been to incorporate into the state what Scott calls the "free gifts of nature" — forests, game, wastelands, prairies, surface minerals, water, and air rights. And this has meant that most once-private natural property is now under the surveillance of the land, resources, and animal police. Recently, after two years of caring for a pair of swans on my pond that might otherwise have become a meal for coyotes, I was shocked to see two smartly uniformed federal officers from Wildlife Canada pull up in a brand-new Jeep Cherokee. They served me with a $240 dollar fine for "keeping swans without a licence" (a $10 dollar fee I had failed to renew). Protestations that it was costing me plenty in food and in bubbler pumps to keep my pond open in winter were for naught. And then, this past spring, in an attempt to purchase a piece of vacant land for a new home and driveway, I was informed by several layers of bureaucracy that the work could not begin until July, "after the birds have left their nests" and that the one thing that would "absolutely stop the driveway" would be the discovery of a butternut tree in its path. My question, asked (I am ashamed to admit) in a somewhat tremulous voice — "Why are my birds to be more protected than my snakes, beetles, turtles, or worms?" — produced a perfectly bureaucratic look of "just wait and see."

By the close of World War II, the macro form of violent fascism that had threatened to throw all of Europe under the jackboot was defeated. One of the main lessons of the conflict was that nature cannot be altered or extinguished by force from above for very long. In professor Rudolph Rummel's bleak review of the various utopian carnages of the 20th century, "Death by Government" (1996), he verified about 50 million military deaths and, in addition, an appalling 150 million legitimate citizens slaughtered *by their own governments*! In short, macrofascism, which started with a respectable reputation — recall that Hitler was Time magazine's Man of the Year in 1938 and Mussolini was the hero of Western cocktail chatter — ended with a very bad name.

Despite the dark failures of the Axis regimes, manifestations of macrofascism as systems aiming to triumph over nature have continued in newer, more subtle, and pervasive ways. No machine-guns have been required, so far, but places like Canada and Sweden are on the brink of becoming — may already be — tripartite states in which one-third of the people work to create wealth and jobs, one-third works for government, and another third receives significant government welfare or other support. Anyone can see that the last two-thirds will always gang up on the first — which is why no artillery is required (all you need is democracy).

So it seems that in a pragmatic response to the collapse of the macro form, a softer microfascism, also rooted in a much earlier intellectual tradition, evolved slowly through the second half of the 20th century and is now in full bloom as our most pervasive and most invisible political religion. It has produced a historically unprecedented type of polity, characterized by a radically individualistic and autonomist ethic that nevertheless rather ironically seeks to organize itself as a

     BEYOND THE RHETORIC

national inventory of common public orthodoxies expressed not as a collective triumph of the will over nature, as in the past, but instead as the triumph of the will of each and every individual over his or her own individual nature.

The most influential prophet of this revolutionary trend was the English philosopher John Stuart Mill, who enunciated most clearly in his canonical booklet "On Liberty" (1859) the notion that liberty — and therefore morality — boils down to doing whatever you want to do as long as you do not harm someone else. It took a while, but Mill's "harm principle," although developed from a number of European ideas (most likely lifted from Article 4 of the French Revolution's 1789 Declaration of the Rights of Man and of the Citizen) slowly began to radiate outwards to infect all Western nations. Today, it operates as a corrosive solvent upon community morality by persuading millions of people that individual freedom of will should be preferred to the common good. So powerful is the appeal of this new individual standard that it has been enshrined into the highest law by Canada's Supreme Court as a replacement for community standards. In Regina v. Labaye (2005), it specifically cited Mill's harm principle as its authority. Just so, the myriad communities of the West seem to be fragmenting into a collection of millions of highly regulated individuals who live within their own private moral bubbles — no need to take notice of anyone else's behavior unless bubbles collide.

In retrospect, it seems as if the deeply revolutionary Christian insistence on the moral freedom of each individual human being has continued apace, but in a mutated secular form especially visible in our tortured skewings of law and social policy to grant legal priority to private will, or "choice." This is ironic, of course, because our spiritual progenitors exercised their free will to escape a slavery to their own bodily appetites and temptations, but we now cite the sanctity of choice as our authority for indulgence in those same appetites. This new war of the will against constraints, especially those on our own biological nature, has taken many forms, and what follows is a kind of fugue on that theme.

Signs of the shift to radical individualism have been visible for a long time, especially in public disputes about "sovereignty," which today has little to do with the admirable Western struggle to establish individual liberty within a politically and morally ordered polity.

Rather, sovereignty, as we now conceive it has more to do with "rights" and with individual claims against the body politic — which is to say, with the demands of the imperial self. To trace this path over past centuries is really to describe a halting line falling from heaven to earth: from God to royalty, to aristocracy (where it is still partly lodged in new and devious forms, such as on our judicial benches), to "the people," and finally ... to the solitary individual.

The British historian George Gooch observed that modern democracy is a "child of the Reformation," because he had traced the rapid transformation of the original Protestant demand for individual spiritual autonomy into a secular demand for political and personal autonomy. This went viral, as the saying goes, rather quickly, in quirky displays of antinomianism. During the English Revolution, for example, discontented soldiers in Cromwell's army actually insisted that the generals should take orders from the soldiers! But Gooch did not live to see the radical expression of this same trend in what may be called our "hyperdemocracies" — political regimes in which, against even democratic logic, sovereignty, and rights are believed to inhere primarily in individuals, rather than in their communities.

"One man, one vote" is now emblematic of the egalitarian democratic faith, but it would have shocked our forebears (who wondered why the vote of an idiot should cancel the vote of a genius) and is an indication of the downward historical trend of sovereignty, which has only come to a halt in our prisons. Voting rights are even granted to convicted criminals in places like Canada, where no one bothers to ask why those who have demonstrated a preference for breaking the laws ought to have the right to determine them.

Another hint of microfascism at work can be seen in social atomization. Aristotle famously declared that we are all *zoon politikon*, or political animals, who naturally affiliate in social groupings. Yet in parallel to the descent of sovereignty has been a startling growth in the "atomization" of the natural social molecule. There are now millions of "administered" individuals, each an entry in bits and bytes on the lockstep computers of the all-seeing state as well as in the electronic files of any corporation that can afford such information-gathering (often purchased from or provided by the state). When I was young, we had a family health card. Now we each have an individual one, a process of individuation repeated in all walks of life,

 BEYOND THE RHETORIC

public and private, and now considered a normal and rational informational requirement of human organization. Although we have never believed more emphatically that we are free, we are individually under near-total surveillance. Consider the spread of the rfid, or "spychip," a tiny "radio-frequency identification device" so small it can easily be placed almost anywhere. It is activated by a radio receiver-transmitter such that when you walk into a government building or your favorite department store the spychip inserted in your shirt, tie, bra, eyeglasses, or blue jeans during manufacture will reveal lots of details on your whereabouts and behaviors. So much for the individuation of bodies.

The real focus of the new micro-war against nature is biology — everything from the skin inward, especially sexual desires, reproductive matters, and, for serious ideological reasons, the ultimate question of the existence or non-existence of human life. In a regime of personal will, it is possible for an ideologically inconvenient "other" to throw into jeopardy the elaborate moral, and legal justifications of the regime itself. Whenever this looms as a real threat, the most urgent question becomes "How can we make the threatening other disappear?" For the truth is that, in order to sustain ideological purity, many regimes in history — we are no exception — have been forced to make entire classes of humans disappear legally. Most Greeks and Romans, for example, simply took for granted that their empires — especially their democracies — were impossible to sustain without chattel slaves whose labors freed citizens to participate in political life. But as no free person can in good conscience enslave another free human being, they had to invent a special category of law that transformed slave-humans into slave-things. My point is that the most egregious ancient as well as modern example of the triumph of the will over nature is human slavery. It is a triumph that simply cannot be sustained without making a target class of natural human beings disappear. Although the transatlantic slave trade was the most obvious recent commercial employment of this repellent art, it is an art still very much in service to the ideological maintenance of our own hyperdemocracies.

We see this slave-making technique in operation today where egalitarian radicals have negated the natural and eternal biological differences between the genders. They have succeeded in arguing that, in order to be equal citizens, women must have the right to triumph over the natural consequences of their own sexual behavior by removing the natural burden of their own unwanted children. This could not be achieved, however, without first converting an entire class of human beings — the unborn — into things. The legal weapon of the ancients was required, and, in order to attain egalitarian purity, democratic nations have legally converted their unborn children into womb-slaves whom they declare to be non-human until born alive.

A physician friend once clarified this technique by asking why, on one side of a one-inch-thick hospital wall, physicians are spending a million dollars on high-tech professional skill to save and preserve the life of a premature baby, while on the other side their colleagues are throwing an aborted baby of exactly the same weight and gestation into the garbage? If, at the right moment, the two mothers were to make the opposing "choice," the child to be saved would disappear and the non-human child would suddenly become human. Clearly, the source of such existential prestidigitation is the naked will of the mothers, by whom human life is created *ex nihilo* or extinguished, not via biology, but by will alone. I am not judging this fact morally at the moment. I am simply trying to present the bald truth that as a political and moral extension of the microfascist will to triumph over nature, the Western democracies, by ideological imperative, have adopted a legal technique for converting millions of human beings into things. Thus have we become slave-regimes of a new kind.

Another looming reality in our aging democracies is the growing clamor — already achieved in some jurisdictions — for the right to control natural death. Suicide is self-inflicted death, but, beyond the understanding that to rest the ethos of a human society on a right of suicide would be to opt for something very dark indeed, we cannot object to nor very easily prevent this use of will. Euthanasia, however, means someone else has to make you die or help you die; someone living must be an instrument in the killing of another, regardless of how remotely. Here too, the will, ever strident, is demanding mastery over nature. In the Netherlands, there is now a group called Out of Free Will campaigning for the right of people over 70 who are "tired of life" to be euthanized. Of course, these campaigns do not address the corresponding obligation upon another (usually an agent of the state) to do the killing required by such a law. The underlying logic

   BEYOND THE RHETORIC

is that just as we can create life or make it disappear in the womb by will alone, we ought to be able to end it by will alone. Just so, the legal right to will a kill, so to speak, is shaping up as the ultimate triumph over nature, because it means openly playing God.

Wanting to be a godlet is not some modern trend; rather, it is an ever-present, and once heretical, human desire. The freedom-loving Adamites of the 15th century, for example, declared themselves to be so pure and god-like they were incapable of sin. Their altered Lord's Prayer began, "Our Father, who art in us," and their passion for adultery they considered a sacrament, good simply because freely willed. In the 17th century, the influential Jacob Barthelmy declared that God "is in this dog, in this tobacco pipe, he is in me and I am in him" (no capital H for egalitarian Gods). Many voluntarists down the years recommended promiscuity and adultery for the "subtle in spirit" whom they encouraged to indulge in a "paradise of the senses" without shame (as in the Garden of Eden), thereby to become "as free as little children once again." One such fellow, Abiezer Coppe, promised all women who fornicated with him would become virgins once again, thanks to the conscienceless purity of his motives (perhaps the craftiest sexual self-promotion ever invented).

Of other biological aspects of nature over which we now seek a mastery of will, there are too many to count. One of them, "no-fault divorce" ("two to make it, one to break it") — considered purely as a social site for the expression of radical will — has clean removed the natural contractual basis of marriage, thus returning us to the radicalism of the French Revolution during which the Jacobins argued that if the two spousal wills are not in accord, no marriage exists. Both the union of marriage and the honest contractual intentions of observant spouses have been subjected to the unilateral "choices" of disaffected spouses.

More of the determination to triumph over nature is apparent in our gender-constructing, gender-bending, and gender-merging discourse, too, not to mention in our choices — in time of conception, in time of birth, in womb, sperm, and egg. The theme here is that there is actually no binding natural order, for all can be altered by will. Perhaps the most tiresome inebriations of anti-biology logic are produced in egalitarian campaigns calling for laws and public funding to impose androgyny upon us; the most devout exponents insist on forcing boys to play with dolls and girls with trucks. On this score, my feminist neighbor finally surrendered in good humor when, after six months of attitude correction of her children, nature came galloping back: she caught her daughter putting her little red fire-engine to bed with a bottle.

In Sweden, where the campaign against natural biology has been in full swing for a half-century, the tax-funded Egalia pre-school invented and now enforces the use of a "genderless" pronoun. An Egalia "gender pedagogue" said (notice the emphasis on the child's Will) that this change gives the children a "fantastic opportunity to be whoever they want to be." Once again, purity of one's own existence is imagined springing from the purity of unencumbered will. In Toronto recently, there was an uproar because two parents insisted on raising their 5-month-old child "genderlessly." Such children, they claimed (same theme) would grow up as "whoever they want to be." And, in a kind of double-header, the international "autonomy rights" movement aims to recognize self-sovereignty even in minor children and would like to see agents of the state enforce such rights against parents. This combines macro- and microfascism in a single initiative.

Another disturbing aspect of the war against nature is modern "multicultural" policy. In the middle of the 20th century, Julien Freund opined that only three things matter in politics: command and obedience; the public and the private; and the insider-outsider distinction. Deep culture is a product of this latter, frankly illiberal, but deeply natural human tendency to bond socially according to widely shared values as insiders creating outsiders. Wherever a deep culture exists and is upheld, people naturally assimilate to it; the modern nation state is a natural expression of this tendency. Rather ironically, then, multicultural policy, which began as an earnest attempt to denaturalize this illiberal fact of life, has turned millions of citizens into cultural microfascists. For as the French critic Pascal Bruckner observed, it has condemned hundreds of ethnicities to "house arrest in their own skins," engendering an isolating "identity politics" that would have made the Nazis proud. In short, multiculturalism has mutated into multi-fascism, a trend that is creating mini-nations within nations, many of which, as in France, are now violent "no-go" zones for police. Nature has come galloping back again.

Just how far does the microfascist trend of extending will over nature go? As far as the entire cosmos, it seems. In 1971, the American astronaut Alan Shepard was sufficiently irreverent to drive a golf ball 800 yards on the moon — a gestural transfiguration of the solar system into a personal playground. But the extension of will over nature extends even farther. In the notorious 1992 Planned Parenthood v. Casey decision of the U.S. Supreme Court, we heard for the first time that *"at the heart of liberty is the right to define one's own concept of existence, of meaning, of the universe, and of the mystery of human life."* This oft-quoted declaration betrayed an utterly unselfconscious confidence and conceit, whereby even cosmic meaning was declared subject to — a creation of — personal liberty and wherein there lurks a right not simply to search for ultimate truth outside ourselves, but also, in a kind of cosmic inversion, to create it within ourselves. It was a pro-godlet ruling that subjected the meaning of all of nature and the universe to individual will, while at the same time pulverizing that meaning into demos-bits.

We may conclude by saying that our view of freedom, and therefore of God, has changed a lot. We used to say that because God is the ultimate Good and can only do good things, we ought to follow suit. Freedom was obedience to the Good. But we have switched Gods to make a more convenient life. We had to, because a regime resting on a foundational ideology of individual sovereignty requires a God of pure will, in whose image we can proceed to fashion ourselves with every personal choice. At such a point, with no constraining external truth, the Good is absorbed into whatever is willed. Will becomes truth, not in the body politic as Rousseau had hoped, but in each individual body, producing our millions of godlets. This switching of Gods constitutes a theological revolution in Western life with profound and as yet unforeseeable implications.

This article originally appeared in The New Criterion, Volume 30, Number 2, on page 18. •

Congresswoman Marcia Fudge holding a T-shirt in 2018.

Source: Wikipedia, https://en.wikipedia.org/wiki/Woke United States

3. Wokeness: A New Religion

JULY 20, 2022

CIVILIZATIONS tend to repeat the ideological pattern that made them strong in the first place. At first, these patterns have theological form and substance. But if belief in God becomes obsolete, they tend to continue the same pattern in secular form, minus religious substance.

To visit my neighbor's home at Christmas is to enter a palisade of tinsel, baubles, winking lights, and lots of little reindeer and elves — but no hint of Christianity to be seen.

A Little Spiritual History

For two millennia, the Christian nations of the West have been nourished and deeply inspired by the expectational vision and promise expressed most notably in the Book of Revelation of a perfect, 1,000-year Kingdom of Heaven to come with the return of Christ. That promise has supplied a deep Western psychological wiring, so to speak, that operates to this day and is plainly heard in the words of the Lord's Prayer: "Thy Kingdom come."

That vision of a perfect future world got really fired up politically by the prophetic end-time outline of Joachim of Fiore, a 12th-century Calabrian monk who taught that all history is divided into three ages. The first is the Age of Law and the Father (all pre-Christian history, a time of fear and servitude), the second, the Age of the Son and the Gospel (a time of faith), and the third, yet to come, the Age of the Spirit (the second coming, and the perfect, 1,000-year Kingdom of Heaven).

"Mille" in Latin means one thousand. Hence, the label "millenarian" as a descriptive term for believers in the Kingdom to come. A complete history of the fanatical religious movements — enormous mobs of distraught, wild-eyed Taborites, Hussites, Adepts of the Free Spirit, Anabaptists, and so many others — who wandered all over

Europe in thrall to one or another prophetic vision of personal salvation through faith in the Kingdom is fascinatingly laid out by Norman Cohn in his landmark study "The Pursuit of the Millennium" (1957). He describes Joachim's third age as an egalitarian time of love, joy, and freedom, in which "God would be revealed directly in the hearts of all men." Directly!

It was, he adds, "the most influential prophetic system known to Europe until the appearance of Marxism."

Eventually, this specifically European prophetism found fertile soil in America, where it was ecstatically expressed in at least four continent-wide "Great Awakenings" (the original form of "wokeness") from the mid-18th century to well into the mid-20th. The first was sparked in 1741 by preacher Jonathan Edwards, who, in a famous fiery sermon, pointed his accusing finger at "sinners in the hands of an angry God." He inspired belief in a deeper piety and a higher standard of personal morality in hundreds of thousands.

This specifically American kind of spiritual awakening eventually took original, sometimes fanatical root in the form of a half-dozen newly invented American religions such as Seventh-day Adventist, Jehovah's Witnesses, Pentecostalism, Southern Baptist, and a few others fascinatingly explored by culture critic Harold Bloom in his eye-opening book "The American Religion" (1992).

Some Disastrous Recent History

By the early 20th century, however, following the catastrophe of World War I, God was increasingly deemed an abject moral failure and got kicked out of the building, especially by millions of disillusioned, grimly atheistic university graduates emerging from the fever swamps of higher learning.

By this time, the soft liberal democracies of the West had been on a path to extensive secularization for more than a century. But the old wiring remained. So if God is really dead and gone, went the thinking, then we have to create the Kingdom on earth by ourselves.

The possibility of a perfect secular world soon became the ideological objective of a lot of Western leaders, but especially of the most vicious modern dictators prepared to liquidate millions of their fellow citizens to achieve it. Soviet International Socialism (Communism) and German National Socialism (Nazism) became the two most prominent European promissory visions of a perfect, socially just world — an end justified by any means.

When, in 1996, after the fall of the USSR with its long history of unspeakable cruelty and the slaughter of so many of its own people, the Russian Communist Party was attempting a comeback by electoral means, Time magazine asked Gen. Albert Makashov if they had anything more specific in mind than restoring Soviet power. He replied: "What is our maximum program? The Kingdom of God on earth — or communism, as we call it — before the third millennium."

Meanwhile, in the middle of the long communist debacle, Adolph Hitler directly plagiarized Joachim's entire historical program (minus God) for his national-socialist Third Reich (German for "third kingdom") which, he boasted to the world, would last "for a thousand years."

That's what I mean by saying the wiring is still very much in place. Both tyrants were following the same centuries-old Western wiring to create a social system so perfect, as the poet T.S. Eliot remarked (of all such promissory systems), that "no one would have to be good."

Our Woke World: A Caricature of Christianity?

Could our present fevered "Great Awokening" be a new, secular form of Puritan revival rooted in the divinity of various group identities (gender, race, sex, class, color, and so on), instead of in individual identity? Does group identity now signal a secular salvation separating the saved from the unsaved?

It would seem so. For we are daily subjected to a myriad of public confessions of group guilt, to the public cleansing of historical group sins, and to a social-justice gospel empowering believers to sniff out previously hidden sin in themselves and others.

The "unwoke" are no longer sinners in the hands of an angry God. They are sinners in the hands of angry puritanical reformers preaching the urgent need for a "Global Reset" (code for the overthrow and remake of Western civilization in its entirety).

There's more. Wokeness comes with its own rigid orthodoxy, and transgressors are considered heretics to be punished immediately, beginning with public demands for penance ("check your privilege"); the casting out of demons ("cancellation" and "deplatforming"); and, of course, insistence on the public right to disturb and instill guilt in large crowds of the faithless, with shows of personal piety by "taking a knee."

Finally, as in former periods of religious public madness and delusion, the remedy for sin is forced confession, recantation, and self-purification of all inherited microaggressions, with the goal of liberating unwoke souls from slavery to their own spiritual blindness.

Then, come the ceremonial defacing and violent mob destruction of statues and paintings of unwoke Western heroes — a direct replication of the Puritan smashing of Catholic idols and altars in the 17th century — while civic employees quietly rename streets and public institutions to purge them of association with past sin, and clear unwoke books from libraries and schools.

Global Wokeness

The new woke catechism has global ambition, and there are suspicions that it's but the cutting edge of a transition from traditional soft Western socialism to a hard totalitarianism that's being accelerated with the help of sweet-sounding, if confused, ideological tools.

The most radical of these is called DEI ("diversity, equity, and inclusion"), a soft-Marxist initiative dividing the whole world into oppressor versus oppressed classes that has already spread like wildfire into every government office, media outlet, digital platform, and corporation in the land as an established faith, and may be seen in documents such as "Global Diversity, Equity and Inclusion Benchmarks: Standards for Organizations Around the World."

Superficially, DEI is a powerfully attractive set of egalitarian notions aiming for the proportional reconstitution of every institution according to, well, the proportions of human beings in the surrounding society at large according to exact ratios of sex, gender, race, class, and so on.

Evidence for failing to achieve an exact proportionality — for example, 50–50 men and women on all corporate and public boards — is searched out in every act of public, private, or unconscious opinion, and all institutions are judged guilty until proven innocent by woke purveyors of DEI who have purified their thought sufficiently to judge and condemn the fallen with an irritating confidence.

Western wokeness began in U.S. universities, quickly spread to Canada, and is now invading Europe, to the chagrin of such as

President Emmanuel Macron of France, who has warned of the moral plague of those universities.

And prior to the Ukraine war, President Vladimir Putin of Russia warned the West that communist Russia had already embraced and destroyed itself with exactly this kind of blindly doctrinaire wokeness.

A New Caste System?

In an extensive analysis, author James Patterson points out in "Wokeness and the New Religious Establishment" (National Affairs, 2021), that "wokeness is the opiate of the elites," and asks whether it has already become a new state religion?

For, until conversion to wokeness, citizens are assumed to belong to what has been described by some critics as a lower, maximally "unclean" caste (because born into "privileges" such as whiteness, masculinity, heteronormativity, cisgenderism, capitalism, colonialism, imperialism, and so on), and so they must engage in endless acts of atonement not expected of the caste of the blameless "clean," who bear a myriad of oppressed identities. Refusal to acknowledge and atone for your caste privilege makes you an untouchable.

Patterson adds, pointedly, that "the hiring of diversity, equity, and inclusion administrators at public universities to oversee the representation of clean identities is akin to those universities hiring priests or rabbis to oversee their adherence to Catholicism or Judaism."

But the United States and many other Western nations have strict constitutional laws prohibiting the promotion of religious belief in public institutions, schools, and universities.

So if the new woke liturgy currently disemboweling educational and institutional life throughout Western civilization is ever judged "a religion" by the courts (as was atheistic "secular humanism" by the Supreme Court in the 1961 case Torcaso v. Watkins), then all public institutions preaching "belief in the divinity of identity, the concept of the woke faith community, … and the moral code grounded in the struggle against oppression," in Patterson's words, may sooner rather than later be in for some big legal and funding surprises.•

Anti-communist Hungarian revolutionaries amid the damaged buildings of Budapest, November, 1956.

Source: Wikipedia, public domain, Jack Metzger

4. From Soft Socialism to Soft Totalitarianism

MARCH 30, 2022

AT a breakfast meeting in Toronto with the late George Jonas — an author of keen insight and perspicacity — I asked him what it was like to live under totalitarian rule in Hungary before escaping to Canada in 1956? I will never forget what he said:

"I thought I was fleeing a disease. But … it followed me!"

This was cause for instant sorrow, and I wept inwardly for my country.

Canada's freedom of speech, action, and thought, limited only by traditional bounds of law and custom, was at its high point during the pre-confederation period, when settlers might never see an agent of government their entire lives. It was lauded most poignantly in 1896 by Canada's seventh prime minister, Sir Wilfrid Laurier, in words that rang throughout the unfree world like a proud and resounding gong: "Canada is free, and freedom is its nationality!"

And that is why I wept. For we simply cannot say those words today.

Canada is no longer the free country it was.

Our proud inheritance of ordered liberty began to weaken around the mid-20th century, when along with most other Western democracies we set out to become what observers variously describe as a welfare state, or a social-welfare state. A form of soft socialism.

But events of recent decades, and especially of the past few years, lead me to state cautiously that free and liberal democracy is dead in Canada, for we have definitively crossed the line between soft socialism, and soft totalitarianism. This is a condition of state characterized by the growth of government at all three levels, huge structural debt that will never be paid off, taxation of everything that moves, and minute, pervasive, and intrusive regulation. Last week an

Ontario wildlife officer came to my home and threatened to fine me if I fail daily to clean up the seeds that fall from my birdfeeder.

But perhaps the most reliable clue that the country has mutated to soft totalitarianism is the growth of pervasive negative punishments. Negative because although there are some recent instances of arrest for defying the law, by and large they specialize in the forbidding of nonconforming thought, speech, and action, in threats to suspend professional licences, in fining, shunning, and firing, in the destruction of reputations, and more, but fall just short of arbitrary physical manhandling, arresting, threatening law-abiding citizens, and carting them off to jail. But we are one step closer.

Last week the COVID police called a friend's daughter who had just returned from a trip to the USA, and peppered her with questions about whether or not her 8-year-old is vaccinated. She answered that her children's health was her business alone, and refused to reply. You know what the official said? She said, "If you do not reply to my questions, I will send the police to your home, and they will use their authority to make you reply."

When we think of hard totalitarianism, we think of machine guns at every corner, of jackboots and gulags, of pervasive government spying, of the "psychiatric" confinement of political enemies for no particular reason, of dissidents and undesirables sent to gulag camps in the north, and the like. For now, I'm still fairly certain the tradition of British liberties and common law, of checks and balances, and the division of powers that is our long and glorious inheritance will make that sort of hard totalitarianism impossible in a country like Canada. Or at least, highly improbable.

But we must be wary, for the softer sort is clearly here already, much of it supported and spread not only by government at all levels, but also by Woke citizens, Woke corporations, Woke universities and schools, and Woke media. It showed up in a militant way just a few years ago. The first stage is the State's effort to persuade via the publication and promotion of "correct" positions on things like abortion (slogans like "my body, my right"), on homosexuality (posters in schools shouting "gay is okay") with the Equity, Diversity, and Inclusion troops invading everywhere. This has all progressed rather rapidly to public edicts and warnings meant to stifle, or deplatform, opposing views; to direct control of citizen speech and thought via

     BEYOND THE RHETORIC

political correctness pressures; to the invention of trigger warnings; to official shaming of youth in schools, and media for non-conforming attitudes contrary to the public narrative; to coerced use of language such as gender pronouns, and even to the forced public recognition as "women" of people who are biological men, or vice versa.

Canada has already moved beyond such soft methods to punishment by way of actual prosecution via phony paralegal bodies such as "Human Rights Tribunals," which are just Soviet-style kangaroo courts given the power to fine offenders, and force conformity and "re-education." Still no prison yet, but close. We used to ridicule the former USSR for doing this. But now they are gone, and we are doing it. George was right. The disease is here.

Three appalling soft-totalitarian initiatives — there are many more — deserve special attention, for they are still with us. The federal government's 2018 Bill C-25 (section 2.2.1.1.) forces corporations "to provide annual reports on their approach to fostering gender diversity on their boards of directors and among their executive officers." This begins with the supposed need for 50 percent females on corporate boards, but soon progresses to demands for the whole diversity "rainbow" encompassing religion, culture, sexual "orientation," economic status, disability, and more, to be represented on every board and management team in the nation.

Personally, I don't care if the board of any company whose products I purchase or in which I invest is filled with all men, all women, or any mix of gender or ethnicity — or height, or weight, or intelligence — as long as the product is good. For that matter, if all board members were trained apes who knew best how to run the company, I would be fine with that, too. But as Terence Corcoran of The National Post put it, with this "initiative" Prime Minister Justin Trudeau and his former Orwellian-named "Innovation Minister" Navdeep Bains were launching "another subversive attack on the corporate model that will change corporations into socio/political operations." He might have gone all the way and said "soft totalitarian" operations. Bains threatened legislation and punishment for non-compliance and said he would use whatever other weapons he may have "in his tool-kit" — a tool kit, already! — to impose "equity" and "diversity" on all Canada's corporate boards.

We note that if this measure succeeds, corporate boards in future will have to comprise 50 percent women (or — because gender is now deemed to be a "fluid" entity — some lower, but equal percentage of people who self-identify as men or women (but who may not be), plus a confused percentage of LGBTQers, transgendered, etc., etc.), 18 percent visible minorities, 14 percent people with disabilities; 5 percent Indigenous people, and so on. What a mess. But clearly, still a soft-totalitarian mess. Here's the distinction: The government has its foot on your life and work, but not yet on your neck.

Private corporations in free societies have never been wholly free, of course. They exist by licence of the State and have been forbidden to do lots of things (such as false advertising) and compelled to do others (like, file tax returns, keep minutes, obey labour laws, etc). But they have never before been compelled by the State to alter their own freely chosen, private, sink-or-swim governance structure, which, given the massive regulatory environment in which they operate, was almost the last thing that made them free and private.

For the record, this law was introduced by the same Justin Trudeau who, when running for power in 2015, said: "Leading [Canada] should mean you bring Canadians together. You do not divide them against one another." And then, in an even more archly hypocritical statement, he added that "efforts of one group to restrict the liberty of another are so very dangerous to this country, especially when the agencies of the state are used to do it."

Another alarm came via the Law Society of Upper Canada, a quasi-government agency that controls the licensing of 60,000 lawyers in the Province of Ontario, when in 2017 it released a mandate that all lawyers and paralegals in the province were required to sign an individual Statement of Principles that acknowledges "their obligation to promote equality, diversity and inclusion generally, and in their behaviour towards colleagues, employees, clients and the public."

This was outrageous and abhorrent to a free society because its specific command was to compel not only the thought and speech of every lawyer in the province on matters with which any citizen may lawfully and morally disagree, but also to compel their private actions, commanding them to *promote* these ideological objectives, even in their personal behavior. Or else. (Like, "We have ways to make you talk.").

Personally, I do not believe that "equality" should be forced upon unequals in anything; nor that "diversity" is necessarily a good thing in a world where unity is crumbling everywhere, and nations fragmenting into hundreds of mini-nations within their own borders. For the truth is you can have diversity within unity, but you cannot derive unity from diversity. Nor should "inclusion" be forced upon people or organizations that don't necessarily want to work, socialize, or associate with those for whom they may not care very much. Diversity and inclusion are in effect weapons in a social and administrative war against the principle of merit that has always been central to free people, and only to them.

And the march from soft socialist to soft totalitarian is picking up pace. The public cannot be trusted to know its own mind. So there must be regulations dictating behaviors, then laws enforcing them, then government spies to ensure compliance, then punishment of offenders. George said that when he left Hungary, there were government agents spying on all citizens who were not Communist Party members. They stood on the street corner outside his apartment, even in the rain, all day long. Every day. And my old friend Martin McGrady, a dirt-poor American who became a world-record holder in track and field, and was raised in a terrible ghetto in Baltimore, told me that on a U.S. track tour to Russia there was a communist spy seated at the end of every hallway, on every floor in his flea-bitten hotel, keeping an eye on him and all other guests (rather, inmates). He said he preferred life in the Baltimore ghetto, any day.

Yet another deeply offensive soft-totalitarian move of the Canadian government arose as a form of coercive bribery, or blackmail. The government floats a "Canada Summer Jobs" program to help hundreds of churches, camps, and many charitable organizations hire extra summer help. This program has coughed up millions every year to fund about 70,000 jobs. But our self-righteous high-school drama-teacher prime minister embarked on, well, outright cash-bribery, denying funding to all organizations that refused to sign an "attestation" (that word, again) to the effect that they support "the Government of Canada's commitment to human rights, which include women's rights and women's reproductive rights, and the rights of gender-diverse and transgender Canadians." The government's website will not accept an application unless that box is checked.

If for moral reasons your organization respects the dignity of all human life from conception, or cannot in religious conscience promote contraception, or because, like the vast majority, it believes that the male/female biological order of the entire reproductive world is natural, and not a matter of choice? Tough luck.

As I said, I doubt a country like Canada will ever get to the citizen-spying stage, or … Oops! I just remembered that Ontario's socialist former Premier Kathleen Wynne hired 175 "inspectors" (aka spies) whom she sent around the province to ensure that business owners were actually paying her newly legislated minimum wage. And I did say it's a long way from soft to hard totalitarianism. But, think about it: We already have speech spies, feminism spies, pay-equity spies, human rights spies, the whole paraphernalia of government "re-education" courses for offenders, and shaming and firings.

It's a long road from soft to hard totalitarianism. And some friends are certain we're there already. But I say not quite, and I will write about the differences between these two conditions soon. But it all starts somewhere, and the road has gotten a lot shorter since my breakfast with George. Canada has put on the soft-totalitarian slippers, and will soon want to exchange them for boots.

Listen for the shuffle outside your door.•

Prime Minister Pierre Trudeau gets a round of applause from Liberal members in the House of Commons after signing an accord with the provincial premiers on the constitutional talks in Ottawa, Thursday, November 5, 1981.

Source: CP PHOTO/Fred Chartrand

5. The Charter at 40:
How Canada Got Re-Colonized

WE are regularly treated to surveys of public opinion about Canada's 1982 *Charter of Rights and Freedoms.* Canadians love it, though the vast majority have never read it. Not a word. The real story of the *Charter*, the reasons for it, and its political and moral consequences are widely ignored.

Prior to our founding, settlers in the colonies that became Canada lived under English law according to English Parliamentary legislation and common-law precedent. Laws made by Parliament were considered the voice of the people, even — *Vox Populi, Vox Dei* — as the voice of God, and therefore the "supreme law" of the land. This is still the case in England, which to this day has no written Charter or Constitution. The overarching message of this long, hard-won British tradition is that the elected Representatives of the people are free to make or unmake the laws of the realm without fear of dictation or limit by any higher power.

In the rising democratic spirit prior to Canada's founding, however, colonists became fed up with control over them by British colonial officials and by bewigged judges of the English Privy Council 6,000 kilometres away. So they periodically revolted to achieve "responsible government." They wanted those who made their laws to answer to the people governed by them.

It wasn't until the •*British North America Act* of 1867 creating the Confederation of Canada that we got fully responsible government, and Canadians began growing their own British-style parliamentary and common-law tradition. The only exception was the civil law in Quebec which continued to rely on the French *Code Napoléon.* At last, Canadians could hire and fire their own lawmakers.

This hopeful regime lasted a mere 115 years. In October of 1980 on CBC Television Prime Minister Pierre Trudeau had already announced his lifelong intention "to constitutionalize a Bill of Rights," and he was prepared to try this unilaterally. But the Supreme Court insisted on consent of the provinces, and after intense federal-provincial deal-making, the passage of The Canada Act 1982 made it very clear Trudeau had succeeded in muscling into existence a French-style Charter of Rights and Freedoms. Why? Because he despised and publicly mocked the English concept of government by a Parliament of changeable Representatives cobbling together laws from their debates, absent any higher guiding principles. And he was unsettled by the idea of ten provincial legislatures making their own sovereign laws which in one province might be in conflict with those of another.

In his first book, "Federalism and the French-Canadians" (1968), Trudeau displayed a Machiavellian awareness that although our founding BNA Act of 1867 was designed precisely to block heavy-handed rule from the top, what he pejoratively called our "checkerboard" federal system might serve as "a valuable tool which permits dynamic parties to plant socialist governments in certain provinces, from which the seeds of radicalism can slowly spread." But who said Canada wanted socialist government? Who said Canada wanted to be radical?

As if blind to the grotesque and bloody evils of national and international socialism that had so recently caused the deaths of millions, Trudeau persuaded himself that "there is a greater need than ever for an enlightened socialist approach ..." But what kind of enlightened socialism was he thinking of? In January of 1969, in response to a question from British students, "What kind of country would you like to make Canada?" he replied: "Labour Party socialist, or Cuban socialism, or Chinese socialism — socialism from each according to his means." So here, barely a quarter century after World War II, we had Canada's Prime Minister striding forth boldly under the red flag of socialism in a nation that had just sacrificed 45,400 of its own citizens… fighting against socialism. No one blinked.

Trudeau understood that the sovereign right of unrestricted law-making by elected representatives was a mark of the glory and freedom of the English system. But to a francophone intellectual, the very idea of a nation without a single supreme legal Code that like a magnet orients all political and moral iron-filings below, so to speak, was abhorrent. He couldn't get out of his mind the mocking observation of Voltaire who, when travelling in England had famously said, "You English change laws as often as you change horses!"

That was true. For the English have always felt local law should reflect local interests. Hence the strict division of central from provincial powers enshrined by the Founders in our BNA Act. But Trudeau disliked British legislative localism, and one day his dislike boiled over when he declared that our elected representatives, once 100 yards from Parliament, were "just a bunch of nobodies." It was a disgraceful thing for a Prime Minister to say about his own Ministers. Ugliest of all to him was the fact that elected nobodies had the unfettered right to create statutes in the name of "the people" which stood as "the supreme law of the land." Too many horses to change. What he wanted instead was a sparklingly clear *Charter* of precise logical principles from which all national policy and law would follow, as the night the day.

Trudeau's lifelong intellectual motto was read every day on a wall-hanging created by artist Joyce Wieland for his home at 24 Sussex Drive in Ottawa, on which were embroidered the words *"La raison avant la passion"* — reason before passion (or above, or over, passion). It was a pithy rendering of his personal Cartesian passion for the crimped belief that the good life can only flow from clear reasoning. Just before he began his personal political campaign to change Canada, he declared: "Reason over passion — that is the theme of all my writing." ("Federalism and the French Canadians," p. 127.)

Trudeau seemed unaware that for the English, this notoriously limiting and controlling Gallic conception of the best way to live had long since been stood on its head by the Scottish Enlightenment philosopher David Hume, who shook all confidence in mere human reason by arguing persuasively that *"reason is the slave of the passions."* It's a tool that can be turned to any purpose and therefore gives a false confidence. A century and a half later, G.K. Chesterton, another Englishman, expressed the same distrust in mere reason when he wrote that "the madman is the man who has lost everything except his reason." They were both warning that rational arguments are usually simplifying and circular justifications for underlying passions and motives. Trudeau was never able to admit this sobering and very practical English truth about himself.

The *Charter of Rights and Freedoms* he all but single-handedly created and dropped on our nation as the new "Supreme Law of Canada" on April 17, 1982, fell on our political system like a guillotine, ending the supremacy of the people in their own Parliament. With the same stroke, and because abstract terms such as "equality," freedom," "rights," and so on are never self-interpreting, he set in motion a long and continuing stream of judge-made personal interpretations of those terms (themselves often conflicting), the sum of which is now described by every lawyer in Canada as "Charter law." In effect, this is law made by unelected judges, each with his or her own personal political and moral persuasion and passion, *who are never directly responsible to the people and cannot be removed by any power in the land*. To this extent, and specifically because elected Parliamentarians today will not presume to create or change a law they fear might be in conflict with some principle of the *Charter* (OMG, what will the judges say? Will this survive *Charter* scrutiny?), Canada's Parliament has been infantilized.

Most judges have taken this new quasi-dictatorial *Charter* role deeply to heart. One example will do. Here is the Right Honourable Madam Beverley McLachlin reflecting on her 17-year role as Canada's Chief Justice: "My job is to think about what's best for Canadian society on the particular problem that's before us, and give it my best judgement …" (*National Post*, May 23, 2015). But that is entirely untrue. It was her job to rule on the facts of the cases before her according to the pertinent law of the land, not to ponder what's best for Canadian society. That's the job of the Representatives we send to Parliament. But she considered herself a progressive politician as much as a judge and ruled accordingly. Had she been of conservative temperament, she would likely have ruled another way. But either way is to be a political activist more than a judge.

The reality of such judge-made *Charter* law means that with one stroke, Trudeau shoved us back into the political condition under which we suffered prior to 1867. In effect, Canadians got re-colonized. Not by a foreign power, but by their own hand. Trudeau was not citing *Magna Carta*, Locke, Blackstone, or Burke as his intellectual teachers. No. He embraced instead the writings of the main French architect of totalitarian socialism Jean-Jacques Rousseau, the inspiration of Marat, Robespierre, and Danton — murdering revolutionists all — who justified all their actions according to Rousseau's conception of "the General Will" (*la volonté générale*).

It was an idea that became Trudeau's personal political and moral mantra. In one of his last publications, "Pierre Trudeau Speaks Out on Meech Lake" (1990), he used the phrase *volonté générale* repeatedly, and inaccurately. He urged Canadians "to create a national will … une volonté générale, as Rousseau had called it." But he didn't understand that a "National Will" — a simple idea born with modern liberal democracy — is something quite different from Rousseau's notion of a "General Will" which is at the theoretical root of all totalitarianism. It was the latter Trudeau wanted to put in place in Canada, and with his *Charter*, arguably did.

What is the difference? A National Will of the people is a headcount of the majority that emerges bottom-up, so to speak, after the heat of debate, and is accepted by winners and losers alike with exceptions, compromises, and disagreements tolerated. A National, or majority, Will may be as low as 50 percent plus one vote, but there is agreement in advance that the losers in such a vote accept the will of the majority. That's what happened in 1995 during the so-called Quebec Referendum on separation. The No side won by a slim margin, and the Yes side went home without starting a civil war. Practical British tradition at work.

A General Will is different. It's a wholly abstract, totalizing concept created from the belief that for any problem concerning all the people, there must be — rationally speaking, *can only be* — one best solution, one General Will for the Common Good. Therefore the General Will is always correct and for the good of all, and once discerned and decided it requires total rule issued as a command from the top by an official Rousseau called the Supreme Legislator (in our case, the Supreme Court). So logically compelling was this idea that in his widely influential "Social Contract" — the Bible of French Revolutionists — Rousseau advocated the death penalty for all who opposed the General Will. It is a notion utterly alien to the British way of life and inherited political history, and in the hands of German and Russian totalitarians of the 20th century it nearly ended Western civilization. Despite these historical facts, Trudeau flirted his entire political life with how to create a single General Will in a Confederation such as Canada, a union structured precisely by our Founders to block the very idea of total rule from the centre. They wanted to block social engineers like Trudeau.

But Trudeau pummelled our Founders. By means of his *Charter*, Canada has been changed, uprooted, altered beyond recognition from its noble beginnings in British liberty. The English under General Wolfe won the Battle of the Plains of Abraham against the French General Montcalm in 1759. But in what must be considered "The Revenge of Montcalm," the French have won the ideological and juridical war for the Canadian mind and soul.

That is the real significance of our *Charter*.

Editor's note: This article was updated on Jan. 6 to add more details about former prime minister Pierre Trudeau's initial discussions of a Bill of Rights in the early 1980s. •

Slavery and Freedom in Niagara; Power and Butler (1993).

Source: Digital Collections. Monroe Fordham Regional History Center, Archives & Special Collections Department, E. H. Butler Library, SUNY Buffalo State.

6.   Canada's Slave Trade

AUGUST 24, 2021

SLAVERY? **In Canada?** How could it be? A little booklet called "Slavery and Freedom in Niagara," by authors Michael Power and Nancy Butler of Welland, Ontario, landed on my desk, and got me going on this subject. In school, we learn only that Canada-the-good served as a kind of Holy Land for persecuted slaves who escaped from a barbaric United States.

This has created an unjustified belief in our moral superiority.

For around the year 1780, there were an estimated 4,000 blacks living in the Canadian British colonies, of whom about 1,800 were slaves. Canada's first anti-slavery law (of sorts), of July 9, 1793, didn't exactly outlaw slavery. It was called "An Act to Prevent the Future Introduction of Slaves." In other words, slavery would remain legal — but no more slaves could be imported to Canada.

Now, it's easy to spring to judgment on all this, until we recall that slavery, practiced at some point prior to this century by almost every known civilization, and defended by Plato and Aristotle as "natural," was until very recently protected by international law. In the 18th century, even freedom philosopher John Locke argued it was morally preferable to the death penalty, which is what many slave captives might otherwise have received. And it's easy to agree that ancient slavery, which was primarily based in the practice of enslaving surrendered enemies who had slaughtered your sons and raped and killed your women, was humane (and profitable) compared to slaughtering them in revenge.

Slavery was widely practiced in Africa for millennia by black tribes that sold blacks to each other, to Arabs, and to whites. The U.S. census of 1830 records that 10,000 slaves were owned by "free men of color." Often, the first thing a freed slave would do if he got enough money was to buy himself a slave. The last nations to outlaw slavery were those on the Arabian Peninsula, in the 1960s!

When Columbus arrived in the New World in 1492, he discovered that slavery was already widely practiced by the local Tiano, Arawak, and Carib tribes, along with cannibalism and torture. Many American and Canadian Indian tribes, such as the Tonkawa of Texas, or the Kwakiutl of British Columbia, had been slaveholders (or cannibals, or both) since forever. At the time of white conquest, up to 15 percent of the Kwakiutl were slaves to their own powerful chiefs. White Europeans who arrived in Mexico were horrified to discover an Aztec civilization built on slavery, human sacrifice, and cannibalism of thousands of slaves per year!

As for pioneer Canada, Power writes that "slave owning was widespread among the emerging political and social elites of Upper Canada." Peter Russell, Matthew Elliott, and many other distinguished men who sat on the Legislative Council of Upper Canada each owned dozens of slaves.

Most sought to protect their "right" to own slaves by arguing that a slave was legally owned property, and the right to own property was basic to all free societies. Courts that took away legally owned slaves could then take away land, or homes, couldn't they? And then tyranny would reign.

Farmers asked who will compensate us for our freed slaves, and the lost benefits from slave labor? Many settlers were Loyalists who came to Canada because the government had promised them cheap land on the condition they clear it. So slaves were purchased specifically for that purpose. The government had lured them. Was the government now going to ruin them?

An irony of the history of slavery in Canada is that many individual U.S. states (Delaware, Michigan, Rhode Island, and Connecticut) had banned slavery outright 20 years before Canada prohibited (only) the future importation of slaves. So the state of Michigan, Power writes, became "an instant haven for slaves escaping from Upper Canada." Canadian slave-owners complained bitterly, imploring our lieutenant governor to stop what was in effect a reverse underground railroad. He refused.

A friend, expressing his instant moral repugnance, asked, "How could they not see the immorality of it?" I replied, "Just like we do not see our own." Slaves were legally defined as non-persons. Future historians will surely wonder at our own tortuous moral and legal chicanery that grants modern mothers the legal "right" to vacuum out — or even crush heads and tear limbs off — young babies in their own wombs? They do this so easily only because an unborn human is defined in our criminal law as a non-person.

Ironically, it's the very same modern liberals who so violently deplore slavery, who as violently defend the right to abortion on demand. They don't "see" their immorality. Neither did slaveowners.

Are we much better off? Physically, in the sense that we're not owned — yes. But if we ask about control, the answer may be less pleasing. In past times, though less than 5 percent were slaves, the average citizen, white or black, was quite free of the countless thousands of meddling laws and controls that deeply invade our persons, property, and privacy — and they had to pay not a penny of income tax.

Yet today, entire populations in the "free world" are tax slaves to massive governments for more than half of every year of their lives — and face real physical imprisonment if they refuse to pay. If you're forced to surrender all your income to government, you're certainly a slave. So then, what are you when forced to surrender up to half your income? Surely the answer is that you're half a slave. Physical ownership of persons isn't necessary to control them.

That's why the American revolutionist Josiah Quincy in 1774 cried out against what was then the very deeply shocking idea of taxing human work: "I speak it with grief — I speak it with anguish … — I speak it with shame — I speak it with indignation — we are slaves."

He deplored chattel slavery of the few, but especially the tax slavery of all.

This article first appeared in The Edmonton Journal in 1996. •

Poster by Erich Ludwig Stahl for the film *Triumph of the Will* directed by German filmmaker Leni Riefenstahl. *Triumph of the Will* (German: *Triumph des Willens*) is a 1935 Nazi propaganda film directed, produced, edited and co-written by Leni Riefenstahl.

Source: Erich Ludwig Stahl (1887–1943)

7. The Triumph of Will Over Human Nature

MARCH 20, 2021

I T'S deeply ironic that while our predecessors thought the most important use of human will was to escape slavery to our own harmful appetites and judgments, "choice" is now cited as the most important moral authority for whatever is chosen. It's as if personal choice makes something good, despite the obvious fact we may choose something bad — bad for ourselves, and maybe bad for others, now or in the future.

For more than a half-century, we have been in the midst of an unprecedented legal war against the traditional moral constraints posed by our own biological nature, especially by childbirth and dying. At the same time, we play it both ways. If we want to behave in ways we know are deemed morally wrong, we simply cite biology as our authority, as if to say we can't help ourselves because we're victims of our own nature.

In particular, we demand freedom for everything having to do with our own bodies, especially with respect to choice of sexual object and appetite, and the so-called reproductive right (by which is meant a right not to reproduce). The latter, for deeply ideological reasons, forces us to confront the ultimate political question of the existence, or non-existence, of another human life located within us.

This is by default the most serious issue for all modern democracies because, in regimes resting on a right to equality and the sanctity of personal will, it's possible for the mere existence of an inconvenient "other" to threaten such rights and bring them crashing down. Accordingly, to defend the ideological purity of their own political and moral commitments, many regimes in history have been forced to make entire classes of human beings disappear legally. We have done the same.

The ancient Greeks and Romans took it for granted that their regimes — especially their democracies — were impossible to sustain without slaves whose labors freed citizens to participate directly in political life. So they invented a special category of law to transform slaves into non-humans, into things, mere property they could buy or sell, beat or kill. This went so far as to argue that a slave could be legally charged for homicide, but not for murder, which requires intent, and only a human being can form intent.

All slave-holding nations and tribes in history, including all indigenous peoples of the Americas, have used similar category law or simple dictates to make a specific class of human beings disappear by judicial fiat and reappear as non-human property. The Nazis, communists, and fascists used category law to make Jews, intellectuals, political enemies, and disfavored artists, among others, disappear and reappear under the official dehumanizing label of the moment.

Our modern democracies are using the same legal deception to make millions of unborn children disappear and reappear as what any honest person must recognize as womb-slaves. It's odd that liberals, keen to deplore the history of slavery, seem unable to admit that our democracies, ostensibly devoted to the protection of the weak, have been making slaves of unborn children by the millions for more than a half-century.

They won't use this term, but will argue that without a law that makes unborn children non-human, democratic equality for women is impossible, simply because the natural burdens of childbearing render women disadvantaged and unequal to men. In an egalitarian democracy, inequality is the greatest sin, so a way had to be found enabling women to triumph over nature by eliminating the consequences of their own sexual behavior. Let us concentrate now on the legal and moral confusion this has unleashed.

A Human Being

In Canada, a human "child" is considered non-human until "born alive." Section 223(1) of Canada's Criminal Code articulates this legal abracadabra precisely, as follows: "A child becomes a human being within the meaning of this Act when it has completely proceeded, in a living state, from the body of its mother."

Then, in subsection 2, we read that "a person commits homicide when he causes injury to a child before or during its birth as a result of which the child dies after becoming a human being."

It's simply absurd to state that a "child" becomes a "human being" after separation from the body of its mother, when we have just stated it's a "child" (understood to be a young human being in every language of the world) before separation. It's also absurd to state that a person commits homicide if this non-human "child" is injured before it becomes a human being — when it's a mere thing — sufficiently to kill it after it becomes human.

Just a question, your honor: If there's no human being in there, how can you injure or kill "a child" who isn't yet a child? And if it is a living child (it must be living before it can be killed, no?), then it must be a human child, right? I mean, we know it's not a living turtle or a flamingo. So, your honor, this is really messed up.

In Canadian civil law, a doctor can extract an umbilically attached but not-yet-human "child" from its mother's belly for surgery, at which point it legally becomes "a human being," perform the surgery, then stick the little human being back in the womb to finish gestation, at which point, it loses its humanity for the second time and becomes a non-human but living thing again.

Magic is the belief you have the power to change one substance into another — lead into gold, for example. Not to be outdone by sorcerers or witches of the past, a judge, with just a sentence or two, can magically change a living, kicking human child in the womb into a non-human lump of something or other (no one is saying exactly what), then, just as magically, can change that lump into an actual human being the moment it's out of its mother. Canadian criminal law has produced a miracle almost as amazing as the transubstantiation of the communion wafer into the actual living body of Christ. The legal mind is really something.

A physician friend once illuminated the delusional nature of this magic by asking why, on one side of a two-inch-thick hospital wall, millions of dollars are being spent to preserve the life of a premature 4-pound baby, while on the other side of that wall his colleagues are throwing an aborted, very human-looking, but legally not-yet-human baby of exactly the same weight into the garbage?

For if, at that moment, each mother were suddenly to reverse her original choice, the almost fully-born human baby the medical team is fighting to save would disappear, suddenly converted by the will of its mother alone to the status of a non-human, a mere thing that happens to be alive; while on the other side of that wall, the squirming but living thing still in its mother and so, legally defined as non-human (although it looks and acts in every respect like a human) and just about to be killed, would suddenly be transformed (converted, mutated?) by its mother's will alone from a human-looking non-human into an actual human being.

The source of this existential magic isn't God, of course, or the suddenly invoked incantation of a mystical spirit. It's a legal fiction conferring life-giving, or life-denying, power on millions of women; nay, on anyone simply born female. Little girls in every democracy grow up knowing they may one day say, "You may live; but you shall die." This is an ultimate power previously assumed to belong only to a god.

It's simply a bald truth that as a political and moral extension of the will to triumph over nature, the Western democracies, fanatically beholden to the ideological presupposition of equality for all, have adopted an ancient technique for converting millions of living humans into non-humans prior to disposing of them, thus converting our democracies into slave-regimes of a new kind. We need to speak this truth in the public square: Any modern democracy using this technique is a slave regime, pure and simple.

Playing God

Another instance of this urge to triumph over our own biological nature — already achieved in many jurisdictions — is the rising demand for the right to control death by personal will. Suicide is self-inflicted death, or "self-murder," traditionally viewed with considerable sorrow and disapproval. But, beyond the understanding that to rest the ethos of an entire society on a right of suicide would be to opt for something very dark indeed, we can't very easily prevent this use of will.

So-called assisted suicide is something else. It means someone helps you kill yourself. They give you the pills, hand you the garbage bag to suffocate yourself, wheel you to the edge of the bridge where you jump, whatever. But you self-administer; you do the killing of yourself.

Euthanasia is very different again. It means someone else takes the terminal step to make you die, is instrumental in killing you. This person must apply, tie, and hold the suffocation bag in place against your reflex struggles (or may have to drug you first); put the pills or pour the killer cocktail down your throat; or stick the needle in your arm. Here, too, the will, ever strident, demands mastery over nature, but in this case, someone else, with your consent, asserts a legal and moral mastery over your nature.

In the Netherlands, a group called Out of Free Will has campaigned vigorously (it's not law yet) for the right of people over 70 who are simply "tired of life" to be euthanized by the state. There's much public discussion of "auto-euthanasia," and the availability of a "last will pill." Dutch statisticians report figures annually for ELWERP (End of Life Without Explicit Request of Patient), that is, for citizens killed involuntarily. There's ongoing argument and outrage on all sides over how many do or don't get killed by the state each year. But it happens, and I figure one such killing is outrageous enough. Seniors in Dutch hospitals who don't want to be killed should ask the doctor to drink some of the orange juice before they do.

The latest sophistication in the Netherlands is the mobile death squad, or "euthanasia on wheels." If out of conscience your own physician refuses to kill you, the state will happily oblige. One phone call and a doctor-nurse team from the End of Life Clinic (which has a network of 140 doctors and nurses country-wide) will appear at your doorstep. You just need to answer their questions properly, and they will put you down, free of charge (actually, pre-paid by the tax and insurance system). You can read their advertisement on their Expertisecentrum Euthanasie website.

I visited the Netherlands once. You hardly see any badly disabled kids or doddery old people there. With the proper democratic rights, you can easily clean 'em all out, and open for tourism with the healthiest, most vital population of tall, robust people I ever saw. At any rate, in all modern democracies, the legal right to Will a Kill, so to speak, is shaping up as the ultimate triumph of will over human nature, because it means freely disposing of life and death; it means playing god.

Just how far does this trend of exerting personal will over human nature go? As far as the entire cosmos. In 1971, the American astronaut Alan Shepard was sufficiently irreverent to drive a golf ball 800 yards on the moon — a cocky gestural transfiguration of the solar system into his personal playground. But the extension of human will extends much farther.

In the notorious 1992 Planned Parenthood v. Casey decision of the U.S. Supreme Court, we heard for the first time that "at the heart of liberty is the right to define one's own concept of existence, of meaning, of the universe, and of the mystery of human life." I'm OK with people asking about the mystery of life. I have asked all my life. Searching for meaning is good. But an individual "right" to define? That's extreme hubris.

This oft-quoted, judicially euphoric statement betrays a dumbed-down conceit whereby the meaning of the entire universe is declared subject to invention by so many billions of individual wills we might as well agree it has no meaning at all. At least, none that matters to anyone other than ourselves. It's a pro-godlet ruling that reduces ultimate meaning to private will.

I conclude by saying that our contemporary view of freedom and God has changed a lot. We used to say God is the ultimate good and can do only good things because that is God's nature, so we ought to follow suit. Freedom was observance of the good, and of human nature in search of the good. But we have switched out gods to make personal life more convenient. We had to, because in a democratic regime no longer resting on liberty and the natural differences to which it gives rise, but instead on an ideology of forced equality and the sovereignty of will, you need a god of pure will in whose image you can proceed to fashion yourself.

So now, with no constraining external truth to worry about (truth is up to you), the good is absorbed into whatever you will. Will becomes truth, no longer something to be searched for, found outside ourselves, and expressed in the body politic, but expressed differently by each of us as an individual godlet. This substitution of gods constitutes a theological revolution in Western life with profound and as yet unforeseeable implications.•

The Genius of Liberty by Augustin Dumont, topping the July Column at the Place de la Bastille in Paris.

8. How Western Social and Moral Life Has Been Radically Altered

DECEMBER 28, 2020

The transition from the 'Four Fs' to the 'Four Gs'

COUNTRIES that undergo a peaceful regime change from free and open to closed and less free, usually do so by accepting the gradual substitution of one set of values for another. They abandon what I call the Four Fs and begin accepting the Four Gs as their new belief system.

The Four Fs are *Freedom*, *Family*, *Free enterprise*, and *Faith*, and these are the essential cornerstones of a free society.

The Four Gs are *Government, Groups, Grants and Grabs*, and *Godlessness*. These are the essential cornerstones of an unfree society and part of the gradual shift of all the Western democracies from free and open to more socialist and closed societies.

You can tell when a country has begun to abandon the Four Fs and has opted for the Four Gs when, instead of more freedom, you get more *Government*; instead of a focus on the natural family you see a focus on politically defined *Groups*; instead of the promotion of free enterprise you get a focus on *Grants* and tax-*Grabs*; instead of the social direction provided by a moral law common for all you get the official promotion of moral relativism and *Godlessness* in schools and the public square (which leaves the state free to direct all things).

There are five contemporary forms of radicalism that have enabled and promoted this change in the foundation of Western social and moral life from the Four Fs to the Four Gs.

Radical Feminism

The first and perhaps most virulent of these is radical feminism, which seeks to overthrow the *order of human biology* by promoting the fantastical idea that the sexes are exactly the same and that any differences in the way they choose to live must result from brainwashing. Or that male and female gender is not natural, but "constructed" and freely chosen. But as Harvard professor Michael Levin once dryly suggested, "any parent who has raised both boys and girls and still thinks they are born the same, has already withstood more evidence to the contrary than any laboratory could possibly provide."

The first mistake, however, is to identify feminism with women, most of whom have never supported it. "Feminist theory," as the insightful British critic Kenneth Minogue put it, "is passionate and salvationist in a way similar to Marxism, to new religious movements, and occult enthusiasms. Academically, it is mostly unsophisticated. A little light generalizing work is followed by polysyllabic decoration and some spray-on indignation."

The Abortion/Euthanasia Movement

The second radicalism is the radical abortion/euthanasia movement, which attempts to end our age-old principle of the sanctity of life, thus to overthrow the *order of love* in society.

Euthanasia is really an extension of the abortion movement (which is better thought of as "pediatric euthanasia"). The "right to choose" to kill someone inside you, a living child, easily mutates into adult euthanasia — the right to kill someone who asserts a right to be killed. Euthanasia was made a legal right in Canada in 2015 and is now practiced by physicians licensed to kill other citizens.

Only too late will we discover that the ultimate form of equality in the socialist state is the right to direct this latest ethic of killing to the elimination of all lives considered not worth living.

Radical Pansexualism

The third radicalism is the radical pansexual movement, of which the homosexual, pornography, polygamy, pro-incest, and now the transgender movements are connected parts. This radicalism seeks to overthrow *the sexual order*, especially the marital order, of western society, which is based on four prohibitions as to the number, gender, age, and blood-relation of legal sexual partners. This was the time-honoured belief that a marriage must be restricted to one partner at a time and that the partners must be of opposite sexes, cannot be beneath a specified age, and may not be close blood relatives.

This is bolstered by the radical notion that "love" is a sufficient warrant for almost any human behaviour because we are all naturally good, and so all consenting sex, with whomsoever and however, as long as there is no harm done to consenting individuals, must also be good, with no concern for harm to the ideals of the larger society. It's a belief that dispenses completely with our 2,000-year-long tradition of attempting to teach the difference between good love and bad love (such as narcissism/self-love, incest love, sexual love of little children, love of uncommitted sex, love of polygamy, love of adultery, and many more forms of illicit love, since normalized).

Educational Radicalism

The fourth radicalism is educational radicalism, and here we have a continuous attempt, as the Swedes put it (when radical elitists in Sweden in the 1960s decided to force a switch from the Four Fs to the Four Gs), "to divest the parents of their authority over their own children." Now education radicals everywhere in the West, who see themselves as "change agents," seek to overthrow *the order of private family authority.*

The connection is from Plato, to Rousseau, to the likes of John Dewey, to teacher-training institutions like the Ontario Institute for Studies in Education in Toronto and Columbia University in New York City. The strategy is to persuade the public that teachers are trustees of the nation's children, not for the family but for the state. It was Canada's Laurier LaPierre who in 1978, intoxicated with the vision of a top-down, redistributive state, declared that "the child is not a family child. He is an institutional child. It is not the school that is the extension of the home, but the home that is the extension of the school."

Soon after, former Calgary Board of Education chairman (and education professor) Alex Proudfoot was more blunt. He told a meeting of astonished parents: "The child is not your child. Canadian children are the property of the state, like our oil, our gas, and our pipelines … it's the law."

Legal Radicalism

And finally, we have legal radicalism, the most powerful of all, emanating from law schools, law reform commissions, and tribunals and charters of every description, all of which are intent upon circumventing the democratic process.

It is the legal fraternity that is rapidly becoming the most powerful wing of the political class, and the reason is that they have figured out how to use legal rather than political means to overthrow what they believe is the dim-witted *democratic order* of a free society.

The chief instrument used in this subtle exercise in Canada is its 1982 Charter of Rights and Freedoms. Formerly sovereign and free legislators are now subordinate to legal dictates based on the Charter with respect to most things in life that really matter. The Charter specifically promotes and entrenches the notion of "substantive" equality (making people equal in real life) rather than the original "formal" equality (ensuring equal opportunity under law for all), and so radical egalitarian judgements and social programs get smuggled in under this mutated definition of equality by unelected judges whom no power in the land can remove.

This is a process that bypasses our formerly free legislative sovereignty and replaces it with a new judicial sovereignty. Canada, and many other democracies now identify whole classes of citizens to be favoured over other classes according to linguistic, gender, religious, ethnic, or other differences, in a blatant form of legal discrimination.

If you want more of this kind of equality, you need more government, and if you want total equality, you need total government.

The School of Athens, a famous fresco by the italian renaissance artist Raphael, with Plato and Aristotle as the central figures.

9. On the Dangers of 'Equality'

OCTOBER 29, 2020

THE question of the day seems to be whether or not equality can be legislated.

The short answer is "yes." Anything can be legislated.

But everyone knows that no two human beings, trees, fish or flowers, are exactly equal. Difference is the rule of the universe.

There are many kinds of equality, too. In his famous work "Republic," for example, Plato argued for equal treatment of the class of slaves, of the class of warriors, of the class of property owners, and of the class of citizens (slaves, women, and foreigners weren't citizens). But he was no egalitarian. He never argued for the equal treatment of everyone. So the larger question is: What kind of "equality" are we talking about? And if the wrong kind, whether it will eventually transform our floundering liberal democracies into the genteel totalitarian sort which, under conditions of sufficient economic and social distress, will mutate into the real thing?

The great liberal dream of the West, however imperfect, is of free individuals acting according to their effort and merit as authors of their own lives and destinies, under an impartial law equal for all. Everyone is born with a different hand of cards; you play them to the best of your ability under the same rules. This is often called "formal" equality, because it makes no distinction between citizens as to class, wealth, sex, race, or anything else. A prince and a pauper must suffer the same penalty for the same crime. It's a principle that has underpinned liberalism from its birth, and it's under widespread legal and political attack.

In place of that noble dream, however, we increasingly see the rise of the perennial anti-liberal nightmare rooted in envy, which begins when whole classes of people begin to believe that the differences between themselves and others are a consequence of systemic-oppression, of something outside themselves, that they are victims of pervasive visible and invisible bias and discrimination. So they line up with hands outstretched to the law and the state, demanding "substantive equality." Which is to say, demanding that their lives be improved by differential laws and quotas aimed at leveling inequalities wherever found, whether natural, inherited, or freely chosen.

The problem with this approach is that laws and quotas promoting policies such as "affirmative action" impose a new kind of official inequality of a kind once found only in the most openly totalitarian states, discriminating in favor of one group that has earned no reward, and against another that has deserved no punishment.

From the failures of ancient Greece and Rome to every modern collectivist nation where this paternalistic ruse has reared its head, it has first been introduced by a power-hungry class of legally trained, militantly egalitarian intellectuals zealously bent on installing by force its version of perfect social justice. Substantive equality — the belief that the power of law must be used to equalize all citizens insofar as possible in the outcomes of their lives — is the rallying cry.

This collectivist form of politics is easily traceable from its earliest root in secular works from the "Republic," mentioned above, to the religious messianism that flourished in the second century of the Christian era through and beyond the Middle Ages, to the millenarianism of the "levelers" in the English Revolution, to the utopianism of those such as Rousseau and Paine in the 18th century, to Marx and Engels in the 19th, and on to their many modern acolytes sheltering today in our media, public institutions, and law schools.

The key element at the heart of perfectionism is the notion that the responsibility for injustice and evil in the world can't have much to do with the behavior of individuals, because all human beings are born naturally good. To many of us still, this remains a natural belief. I recall being deeply outraged when the priest who baptized my first child asked God "to banish the devil from her heart." My beautiful, freshly born child a devil? I did have a belief in innate human goodness, but I figured that after a while we choose badness or goodness ourselves.

Utopians, however, are forced by their own logic to reject personal responsibility for badness so they can blame something outside themselves, usually bad social and political institutions and beliefs. The modern high priest of this "something made me do it" tactic was

Jean-Jacques Rousseau, who laid the foundation for this unnatural idea in the first sentence of his widely influential book "The Social Contract" (1762): "Man is born free, but is everywhere in chains." It was a childish and manifestly false notion, for any sensible person knows we are not born free. We are born completely helpless, dependent on loving parents, and bonded socially in our communities under viable laws and institutions formed long before our birth, and the vast majority of us become unchained, free, and independent as we mature.

You can see the contrast with the dominant traditional (and Christian) view that evil isn't a force outside us. It begins deep in the hearts and minds of men and women — of which evil governments aren't the origin, but the reflection. Aleksandr Solzhenitsyn, who suffered great evils in the gulag, and powerful temptation to become evil himself by helping his guards for rewards (which, hungry and weak, he struggled to decline), produced a striking version of this view when he wrote that "evil does not run between human groups. It runs through the middle of every human heart."

Once the comforting view that evil is external and systemic is embraced, however, the logical course of action is to eliminate every external evil by force of law. For this belief you immediately need targets for elimination — usually entire institutions you believe create systemic inequality, and of course, all individuals who disagree with you. If by any means available we can make the world more equal, is the belief, then the natural goodness of all people, their true selves, will naturally flourish, and society — the state — will be perfect.

Whether ancient or modern, this sort of fanaticism — which has become a secular "political religion" in our midst — is driven by a mission to create heaven on earth. Even if you have to pack a court to do it. I remember when the USSR fell, Time asked a Soviet marshal, "Why? What were you trying to do, locking your people up, forcing totalitarianism on them with machine guns and gulags?" The marshal answered, "The Kingdom of Heaven on earth, in the Third Millennium."

Ironically, the more atheistic such missionaries, the more spiritual or dream-like their fervor. For if God is really dead, we will have no help. Justice will have to be defined and enforced by humans alone. The new godhead of this secular religion isn't grace, or personal redemption, but real, tangible, *forced* substantive equality, to be provided by law as dictated by the priests and priestesses — the new godlets — of the progressive state.

For such minds, the end will always justify the means. The famous "Declaration of the Rights of Man and of the Citizen" that set its stamp on the bloody Terror of the French Revolution began by declaring freedom and formal equality (only) a right of all citizens. But as French historian Claude Quetel writes in his recent blistering condemnation, "Crois ou Meurs" ("Believe, or Die"), in less than six months this noble liberal standard mutated into an envy-based public rage against all privilege and a demand for substantive equality. At this very point, the heads of the privileged, the rich, and the successful began to fall to lynch mobs who paraded them, eyes agog and dripping blood, on pikes through the streets of Paris.

"The people" had become evangelical believers in Rousseau's gospel that citizens who fail to follow the general will of the state for their own good must be "forced to be free." Death for unbelievers was his suggested remedy. Believe, or die. His key disciple, Maximilien Robespierre, applauded the death of a quarter-million French citizens in the name of this kind of "equality," which he described for all to hear as "virtue."

In a chilling speech on May 7, 1794, he stated: "The basis of popular government in time of revolution is both virtue and terror. Terror without virtue is murderous, virtue without terror is powerless. Terror is nothing else than swift, severe, indomitable justice — it flows, then, from virtue."

This same purifying incantation is easy to find in all subsequent revolutions, in the words of Lenin, Stalin, Mao, Mussolini, Hitler, Castro, and Pol Pot, all of whom relished murdering millions of their own citizens in the name of equality. Believe, or die.

This terrible truth led the French writer Anatole France to observe that when one starts with the supposition that all men are naturally good and virtuous, one inevitably ends by wishing to kill them all! That's because, by definition, as the drive for righteousness defined as substantive equality rapidly intensifies, no one can possibly be good enough, or equal enough. So the bad (who must be more loosely defined in order to widen the net for virtue as death) are soon labeled internal "enemies of the state." First the privileged aristocrat is targeted; then the baker who dared to sell him bread. Contact-tracing with a vengeance!

Eventually and swiftly, all internal enemies suspected of even the slightest privilege must be suppressed, silenced, fined, sent off to prison, or liquidated as an offender to the principle of Holy Equality. After all, killing is the most logical and cheapest way to achieve perfect equality and social justice, neither of which can ever arrive because they get continuously redefined as still to be obtained (because nothing in life or nature is equal). That's why all egalitarian revolutions end by eliminating even their own founding theorists who are eventually deemed not sufficiently virtuous. That's why even Robespierre, the first grand theorist of the Revolution, "the incorruptible," lost his head, too. He walked dazed, bruised, and beaten to the guillotine, clutching a copy of Rousseau's "Social Contract" to his breast.

I don't wish to suggest for a moment that Canada, or the United States, will ever reach such a point. But no one thought Germany would, either. In fact, Hitler was admired by a lot of prominent Western progressives as the great social and political renovator who single-handedly raised Germany by its own socialist boot-straps. It's rather sobering to consider that the two largest professional membership classes of the Nazi party in its heyday were educated teachers and lawyers.

Just so, our universities, originally a monastic type of institution now secularized, are increasingly resorting to the specific habits of mind that produce the evils of which I warn, and it would be gross self-deception to believe we will somehow be exempt from the worst natural consequences of such thinking. Once a bastion of liberty, the universities of the West have become islands of ideological oppression. More than one observer in history has pointed out that when fascism comes to America (and, I venture to add, to Canada), it will come in the name of democracy.

To conclude, I would say that the current notion of "substantive equality" has become a modern substitute for the leaven of divine grace, or as that astute thinker D.H. Lawrence once described, a kind of "earthly bread" to be gathered up by our priesthood of social engineers and redistributed as "heavenly bread" to thankful, docile masses.

Postscript

This article is a lightly edited first part of an unpublished speech I delivered to 400 students and professors at the School of Law, Queen's University, Ontario, on March 1, 1994, in debate with Sheila McIntyre, then a well-known radical-feminist law professor.

The debate drew a full house, with additional loudspeakers set-up outside the venue, where a gauntlet of protesters advertising themselves as "sponsored by the International Socialists" lined both sides of the walk, waving placards demanding "Protest Speech by William Gairdner, Author of 'The Trouble With Canada,' and 'The War Against the Family.'" I have hung that poster on my wall.

In discussion after this talk, shouts of derision were raised twice. The first time was when (it was 1994!) I told the audience that "one day soon, Canada will legalize gay marriage." It was legalized as a Charter right, although not mentioned there, 11 years later in 2005.

The second cause for loud scorn was when I said, "One day soon, Canada will legalize euthanasia, and license doctors to kill." This drew more loud gasping and shouts of "get serious" from the audience. Euthanasia was subsequently legalized in Canada in 2016 under the euphemistic label "Medical Aid in Dying," on the Charter ground (where it isn't mentioned) that all citizens have a "right to die." But that is silly. Dying can't be avoided, whether you believe you have a right to it or not. The bill was about the legal right of some to kill others.

Perhaps the most telling moment of the entire debate was when I told the assembled students that even though many of their professors were present, students shouldn't be afraid to show their hands on a very important question. Namely, "In your four years here, have you ever been afraid to say what you really think in a class at Queen's?"

About 40 percent of the audience tenuously raised their hands.

The difference between then, and now — after all, we are more "woke" — is that today many of those professors would put up their hands, too.•

A romanticised 19th-century recreation by James William Edmund Doyle of England's King John signing the Magna Carta at Runnymede.

Source: A Chronicle of England, Wikimedia Commons, public domain.

10. Celebrating the West

WITH COVID-19 spreading everywhere, these are unsettling times. All of us are self-isolating and cut off from the normal routines of social life and work.

A byproduct of this unsettling new reality is that we are being more or less forced to spend a lot of time alone with just ourselves. But that's not so bad. Actually, it's an opportunity to reflect a little more deeply on the meaning of our lives, and in the midst of so much uncertainty to be thankful, even to celebrate who we are and what defines us as a people.

In my previous two articles for The Epoch Times, I took aim at how modern multicultural and globalist policies have been undermining the deep-culture distinctiveness of the West in an effort to persuade us — even to shame us — into believing that who we are is nothing special.

But I say enough is enough. The insightful U.S. critic Irving Babbitt warned 100 years ago that if we forget who we are, if a civilization begins to drift, the direction is always downward. So I have decided to fight back, and do my bit to stop the drift.

In this article, I want to celebrate some of the precious gifts of our civilization, without apology. Because no matter how you look at it, from ancient times until now — shortcomings, mistakes, and disasters notwithstanding — our system for producing human flourishing is plainly one of the most successful ever created.

Our Great Political System

Let's begin with the fact that with the exception of the Roman Peace that lasted more than two centuries (27 B.C. to 180 A.D.), no political system in human history has ever produced as successful a combination of national and international peace and prosperity within and between nations sharing the same system.

It's basically a freedom system bounded by policy and law that, with a vulnerable reliability, guarantees lawful individual liberty, specified rights to private property, free association, more or less free speech, lawful free enterprise, regulated trade, defendable borders, and equality before the law. The various totalitarian attempts to replace this system with dictatorship, whether of the national socialist (fascist) or international socialist (communist) variety, have consistently produced chaos and death for millions, and disaster for themselves.

And when it comes to the longstanding dream of all people to exercise some control over those who govern them? The modern Western system culminates in the most important and hard-won right of all — unbelievable, actually: the right to "throw the scoundrels out." And oh, what a beloved right that is! It's the people's bloodless mechanism for correcting their own and their leaders' past mistakes and starting afresh; for counting heads instead of breaking them; and a precious gift of our ancestors, to be venerated.

We forget too readily that this right, in turn, is rooted in the most revolutionary idea of all: that the people *have rights and duties that are independent of whatever human rule — or ruler — under which they happen to find themselves.* These rights are grounded in human nature, and in our specifically Western familial, moral, and religious convictions, as enshrined in our constitutional documents, common law, and traditions.

These began as a claim and ideal of ancient Greek and Roman "natural law," as reflected in dramatic works such as Sophocles's "Antigone," and as spelled out so clearly in the philosophical works of such as Cicero.

They then spread as a Christian ideal, where we learn that this kind of law is "written on the heart." This was, in turn, brilliantly expounded by Thomas Aquinas in the 13th century (and by Hugo Grotius in the 17th) as the first international "law of nations."

Perhaps the crowning legal achievement of the West is the belief — much maligned by modern progressives, but lying deep in our legal tradition — that natural law is above, and superior, to mere human law, and so when the former is transgressed, the latter must be held to account. Aquinas taught that "lex iniusta non est lex" — "an unjust law is not a law" — and therefore, though it may be called a law, isn't morally binding. It was precisely his natural-law standard that was invoked by the judges at Nuremberg to convict Hitler's henchmen who, but for this, would have been freed of all war crimes. The judges laid it down that a mere human law loses all obligatory power if it violates the generally recognized principles of international law, or the natural law.

Further, and despite all that may be reproached of our unique and intentionally limited, checked, and balanced Western political system — whether a republic such as the United States of America, or a constitutional monarchy such as England and the modern nations that began as her colonies — our right to express our individual views through elected representatives, who, in turn, are checked by a loyal opposition (in the monarchies), or by an alternatively loyal or disloyal one (in republican systems, such as in the United States), and by a region-based senate system (so that majorities cannot trample minorities) ... why, the whole jumble is a superior crowning glory that's served as a legal and constitutional repellent of dictators and despots for centuries.

Our Great Legal System

Basic English individual liberties and rights to protection from arbitrary power and state interference were enshrined in the Magna Carta in 1215, and though always under threat and with a precarious endurance, have been defended and improved ever since.

Ronald Reagan was correct: "Freedom is never more than one generation away from extinction."

It needs criticism and ongoing improvement, but as compared to the legal systems of other cultures? No contest! To just a handful of jurists and political philosophers of the British tradition (think of the enormous and continuing influence of Edward Coke and of Blackstone's "Commentaries"), and to many fine jurists since, we owe our powerful arguments against excessive statism, as well as the myriad common-law rights we too often take for granted, including respect for life as reflected in our harsh laws against murder, arson, rape, and even suicide (which used to be called self-murder).

The historian Alan Macfarlane has shown that as compared to the late arrival of such rights in other nations, the English people and all those nations spawned by England have enjoyed specific rights to private property and inheritance since the 12th century, hundreds of years before those living in other cultures (many of which even today do not have such firm rights).

On top of all this is the right to be presumed innocent until proved guilty (summed up in "Blackstone's ratio": "It is better that ten guilty persons escape than that one innocent suffer"). And to be judged by a jury of peers or an independent judge, with a right of appeal to a higher court, is another constitutional gift of our ancestors.

As mentioned, other than Rome at the height of her glory (from whence the West has absorbed much in the way of legal practice) no other system has ever provided citizens with such a cornucopia of legal rights and freedoms. The practical reality is that in all nations that have thrown in their lot with the West, citizens are presumed free by birth and by inherited right, and the main function of law is not to tell them what they must do — the totalitarian preference — but only what they can't do.

There is a huge difference between a law that says, "Go anywhere you want, but stay off the grass," and one that says, "You are only allowed to walk on public sidewalks." Western citizens must stand proudly in defense of their liberty-based laws and rights. They are products of a unique and highly particular inheritance and civilization, like no other.

Our Great Freedom System

Especially to be praised are what I call "the tools of freedom and wealth creation," bits of which have arisen sporadically in other cultures. After all, most human beings are natural traders. But as a complete system? Only in the West. On this note, the word "capitalism" should be mothballed, simply because it's too often a slur-term of the left.

All private and public systems employ capital to advantage, including totalitarian ones (in fact, they love capital. They just don't want you to have any). The real engine of our economic success is not capital. It's "free enterprise."

Compared to all other systems — communism, socialism, fascism, and yes, even so-called democratic socialism Bernie Sanders-style (all of which are top-down statist systems) — ours is quite amazing. Its focus is the flourishing of free individual initiative under the same rules for all. It's a system that supplies the ordinary citizen with largely unrestricted free choice in daily commercial life with respect to how to spend the fruits of personal labor and invention. It's a kind of "dollar democracy," under which millions of very ordinary people voluntarily make or break those who serve their needs and wants.

Notwithstanding the huge debt burdens carried by so many democracies, and the fact that all government debt is really deferred taxation, what I have called our Freedom System is still mostly that.

It's a superior system of free enterprise, private property rights, common-law rights, contractual rights, equal justice for all, protection against force and fraud, and investment opportunities large and small that enable the vast majority of people to freely guide their own lives economically, to their own ends, by their own means, in a culture more or less free of normative corruption. It's a superior, universally-duplicable system that we owe … to what? To our unique cultural history and those who fashioned it, and to nothing, and no one else.

No other culture in the history of the world has ever produced a system as successful. And that's why so many other people have been adopting our system.

Our Great Philosophical, Literary, Aesthetic Tradition

The contributions to human life, understanding, and enrichment by many other cultures have of course been impressive in their own right — Asian, African, Indian, etc. — and are properly and vigorously to be celebrated by those raised in their embrace. But they're not my culture. So, like billions of others, I am ineradicably biased in being able authentically to discuss and defend only one deep culture — my own.

In my 20s, I lived in France for a year — "vive la différence!" I loved it, and am still fluent in French. I also lived in Japan for a half-year, and loved that, too, and can still speak a little Japanese. But I got hooked by luminous feelings of Western origin very young when singing solo parts to Handel's Messiah, and reading moving poetry, plays, and novels by great English authors.

You don't possess a deep culture. It possesses you. I remember so clearly a cold winter's night lying in the dark on my futon in Tokyo, thousands of miles from home, listening to my little pocket radio. I was trying to understand a little of the Japanese chatter and music a bit alien to my ears, when suddenly, I got hijacked by the West. A heart-achingly mournful "fado" song by Amalia Rodrigues, a famous Portuguese singer, simply claimed me. I was overcome by a sudden powerful emotion as the West and all it meant in my forlorn night took possession of me. Soul-penetration. A piercing of the heart. The next morning, I booked a ticket home.

The first thing I did when I got back was to find a recording of her song.

For many reasons — too many to recount here — I am persuaded that the cumulative human search for goodness, truth, and beauty in our tradition is unique (as are all traditions, after all), something to marvel at and defend, and that the recent root and branch attack upon it — mostly by privileged, overeducated progressive radicals wandering in a riot of sanctimonious repudiation of all things Western — ought to be energetically rebuffed. That's what I am doing.

I have tried to find equivalents to the work of the greatest Western artists, thinkers, and writers, only to conclude — and I enjoy vigorously debating this point — that when we consider the whole 2,500-year span, there is simply no other civilization past or present that has produced works of the human mind and heart — of philosophy, literature, music, and art — quite as grand and fruitful of human flourishing as those of the Western tradition.

From Plato and Aristotle, to Augustine and Aquinas, to Descartes and Kant, and onward; from the indelible beauty of the King James Bible to the soaring architecture of Westminster and Chartres, angelic choir voices descending; to the glorious music of Bach, Beethoven, Mozart, Handel, Tchaikovsky — and so many others; to our great English literature, from "Beowulf," to the "Canterbury Tales," to the incomparable works of William Shakespeare above all, whose turns of phrase and genius are simply inexplicable and a gift to all mankind; to Keats and his "Ode to a Nightingale," Hopkins's "The Windhover," Stevens's "Sunday Morning," Yeats's "Among School Children," and for me, in the embodiment of a dreamy mythic childhood on a farm, Dylan Thomas's "Fern Hill":

Time held me green and dying / Though I sang in my chains like the sea.

And of course, let us include all that other very fine French, German, Italian, and Spanish literature over the ages, and more, old and new, all the fine poetry, and the novel form, from Cervantes, Fielding, Dickens, Tolstoy, Balzac, and Dostoevsky, to Joyce and Faulkner, Lawrence, and Mann (I haven't kept up with the moderns).

And then, all those gorgeous sculptures and paintings — the stunning Winged Victory of Samothrace (by an unknown Greek artist two centuries before Christ. Unknown! At a time when no other culture had anything comparable. Not even close). And then … Michelangelo's gorgeous statue of David, the ceiling of the Sistine Chapel, the Pietà, and all of Rembrandt, Turner, much of Van Gogh, many of the French Impressionists, and yes — a lot of Canada's fine Group of Seven — so much stunning painting and sculpture.

I simply can't look at Rodin's mournful work "The Burghers of Calais," without feeling the personal agony of those chiseled subjects, frozen in their painful beauty. Oh, my heart.

And, of course, our lofty English language — of all languages, the most ample, most flexible, the most free and open to innovation (because the least policed!) — has, especially because of our culture of adaptive freedom, become the new "lingua franca" of the entire world.

Open and ample? I once heard a famous professor of French linguistics in a Stanford University lecture boast that he could find all, or part, of every word of the French language, somewhere in the English language. Flexible? Resourceful? No language has over the past millennium absorbed and made its own so many thousands of words from other cultures.

"The Oxford English Dictionary" is a record of this vast process. It's still the largest and most astonishing glory of all the world's dictionaries, the miraculous endeavor of its assembly after more than a century of freely contributed labor by language-lovers all over the world, a signal tribute to one people's love of their culture and language.

Our Great Judeo-Christian Tradition

At the root of all cultural and moral systems a distinct theology may always be discovered, even if buried, camouflaged, or frozen, so to speak. Even anti-God secular humanism boasts of itself as "a religion" ("Humanist Manifesto," 1933).

So here, I will only say that despite so many faults and wrong turns, burnings, crusades, and so on, the theology of love and moral self-examination, we find at the heart of Christendom seems quite fundamental as the basis for a sound national culture and morality. I like the Christian insistence on individual moral responsibility, on the sacred right to life of all human beings (though, in recent times, for adult convenience, almost all nominally Christian nations have denied this to the unborn), on the essential goodness of creation, on the equal liberty and rights of all, and on the call for universal love.

Indeed, the notion of individualism itself, as historian Larry Siedentop has shown in "Inventing the Individual" (2014), has arisen not from secular liberal theorists, as most of us have been falsely taught, but from the universalism first preached by Saint Paul and subsequently developed by the Canon Lawyers of the Middle Ages. Even modern democracy has a root in the councils of the Christian church. It was Innocent III who stated at the third Lateran Council in 1215: "That which affects all should be decided by all."

How unusual and unprecedented, among the nations of the world, that was.

Perhaps the most politically relevant aspect of Christendom from its very beginning is the foundational belief attributed to Jesus himself, that we should "render unto Caesar the things that are Caesar's, and unto God the things that are God's" (Matthew 21:21). Even diehard atheists and libertarians ought to love him for that. That's another foundation of the natural law ethic described above, a saying that, for as long as it survives, drives a wedge between free people everywhere and all totalitarian forms of power, past and present.

Jean-Jacques Rousseau, one of the architects of modern totalitarian ideology, hated Jesus for saying that, because it created what he called the "two heads of the eagle" of power, blocking the unity of state power by calling it always to account.

This is surely the chief political legacy of Jesus to all mankind — and one invoked almost solely by citizens of the West. It stands all political power on its head by turning the governed into perpetual moral judges of their governors. I don't think the democratic systems of the Western world, so many centuries in development, and regardless of how secular they may be today, could have evolved in the way they have without that original admonition.

Because Christianity is uniquely rooted in a belief in absolutes — which is to say, in the existence of discoverable universal truth — we have been culturally gifted the belief that we live in a universe of profound (and discoverable) meaning. This belief has, in turn, unleashed a cornucopia of near-miraculous scientific and technological development, for the reason that no people or culture will search for absolute truth if they believe there is none to be found. It explains why so many other cultures rooted in other theologies have never developed much, or have lain dormant for centuries, only now importing or copying the vibrant technologies and inventions of the West.

In terms of worldwide patents[1] issued on a per-capita national basis, nations of a Judeo-Christian origin dominate.

Beginning with the University of Bologna in 1088, Christendom was responsible for the creation of the world's first true universities, and for a great many of the best universities since, for many of the world's great hospitals, and, of course, for countless national and global charitable organizations. The Christian communities and citizens of the West tend to be universally more freely charitable[2] than their secular counterparts in the West, or anywhere else. I say "freely" because they give of their own free will, and aren't commanded to do this by state or church. A great many of the private international organizations that help the poor and less developed of the world are also of Christian origin.

In these, as in so many things, the West, my deep culture, has never had an equal — and it still doesn't.

This is a truth of which to be proud, and to defend.•

---

1   See: https://www.techrepublic.com/article/the-10-most-innovative-countries-in-the-world/

2   See: https://www.hoover.org/research/religious-faith-and-charitable-giving

**The Monument to Multiculturalism in Toronto, Canada.
Four identical sculptures are located in East London, South Africa;
in Changchun, China; in Sarajevo, Bosnia; and Herzegovina and in
Sydney, Australia.**

Source: By paul (dex) from Toronto — reachUploaded by Skeezix1000, CC BY 2.0,
https://commons.wikimedia.org/w/index.php?curid=9476840

11. The Multiculture Mess: Attacking the Nation-State

IN my last article for The Epoch Times, I proposed an essential distinction between a *deep culture*, such as manifested in political systems, theology, language, art, literature, and common moral beliefs, and a *skin-deep culture*, such as we experience everywhere in the West these days, in things such as the enjoyment of Japanese sushi, French perfumes, German cars, Italian shoes, and American digital gadgetry.

Skin-deep cultures are a matter of consumption, and are enjoyed as such. We purchase bits of them, enjoy them, try new ones, switch tastes, and move on. But deep cultures are profoundly different. We live in them, and they in us, for life.

It's almost impossible to get rid of your deep culture, because it's not like a T-shirt, changeable at will. The special customs, laws, traditional beliefs, and ways of life of all deep cultures form an indelible, and indelibly particular, identity for those raised in their grip, producing in every citizen what D.H. Lawrence described as an indelible "spirit of place" that lasts for life.

You can take the trunk and branches of your deep culture elsewhere, but the roots remain where they grew. Even for those who have left their deep culture to assimilate another, this goes very deep. Psycholinguistic studies of seniors who have learned and lived in a second language all their adult lives but are losing memory, show that the last thing to go — and sometimes the last words they will ever speak — are spoken in their first language.

Skin-deep culture is something we enjoy but can live without. Deep culture is something we will die defending, if we must.

However, despite the crossover things they may share, many deep cultures of the world are profoundly incompatible. They have incompatible notions of God, of family, of law, of political systems, and of correct moral behavior.

Because of this particularity — which the international system of nation-states was created to protect with national borders, rights, international law, and treaties — the political and moral principles of many deep cultures do not sit well with those of another. In this sense, diversity divides.

With the globalist weakening of the modern nation-state ideal, we are seeing more of what political scientist Samuel Huntington described as the "clash of civilizations." The traumatic sight of people jumping to their death from the Twin Towers was and remains a terrifying symbol of this fact.

The Rising and Declining of Civilizations

Civilizations are never stable. They're always either "rising" or "declining." Rising civilizations defend and celebrate themselves, while declining ones are mostly self-critical, laying down their cultural arms to ignore, demean, or even shame their own history. At this point, the public square is dominated by people the late philosopher Roger Scruton aptly described as *oikophobes*(people who hate their own national home).

But civilizations that strip themselves of their own deep culture to embrace a skin-deep one do so at precisely the point when dying for their own deep culture becomes unthinkable. Then they are vulnerable to a bully culture in their midst raising itself to dominance.

This laying down of cultural arms in the West is most easily seen in our ubiquitous "multicultural" policy, something invented by globalizing progressives in a desperate ploy to raise up what they themselves have been lowering.

It rests on the unexamined belief that conflict within and between the nations of the world can be eradicated by persuading citizens to switch loyalty to an international skin-deep culture in which all can share, but which belongs to no one. The ideological linchpin sustaining this belief is the demonstrably false assumption that all cultures of the world are of equal value, and therefore, that a skin-deep mixture — a kind of sampling menu of the week — will do as loyalty-bait.

The weakness of that belief is that it renders declining cultures more defenseless when faced with rising ones, because if all cultures are officially deemed equal, a bully-culture is not easily challenged.

And of course, lowering one's culture (to make it equal to all other cultures) amounts to surrendering the idea that it was ever something unique, moving, formative, and worth celebrating, preserving, dying for, and therefore (oh, the shame of it!), privileging over other cultures.

In short, the transition from a deep to a skin-deep affiliation with one's own civilization is also the moment of the loss of privileging, and so of the will to die for it.

Embracing Multiculturalism

Canada was first in this peculiarly Western race to the bottom in 1988, with a blaring, if logically self-contradictory, national campaign advertising "the world's first Multicultural Act." It was a policy created in response to looming problems common to most democracies then, and now.

With the advent of the pill, and of abortion as a form of contraception, they almost overnight became contraceptive nations, failing to replace themselves naturally. But the very first sign of a declining civilization is when fornication replaces procreation as the dominant sexual interest of a people.

Accordingly, all the Western democracies were soon faced with aging workers, a shrinking tax harvest from fewer young, and higher health care costs for a burgeoning cohort of seniors. To survive and thrive, if they were not simply to plunder each other for new citizens, they would need massive immigration from … non-traditional sources.

But as a direct consequence of importing so many culturally alien immigrants, they began struggling with extreme dislocations (such as foreign gangs, terrorist bombings, and the growth in their midst of urban "no-go" zones), on top of the considerable added costs of cultural, moral, language, and religious adaptations in hospitals, schools, and public spaces. These are clashes between civilizations within nations states, rather than between them.

Multiculturalism was supposed to end that. Canonize the concept, and pass off this new, tolerant, but embarrassingly skin-deep mixture as a universal replacement culture. Give up, to join up, was the plan. But it was a cover-up. I was going to say that no one was fooled. But in fact, most were. Because no one was asking: What might be the downside of citizens abandoning a lifelong love of their own deep culture for a frivolous attachment to a global, skin-deep one?

Here's just one: Multicultural policy has consigned to forgetting and oblivion, nay, has all but shamed, the unifying deep culture that made Western civilization — Christendom, as it used to be called — so remarkably open and tolerant in the first place. Which is to say, with some irony, tolerant enough to make possible the multicultural policy that is presently undermining the West by trivializing our deepest motives for living together.

But a people that neglects to be vigilant, to remember, privilege, and teach the deepest sources of its own tradition and history, will soon be vulnerable to bullying by those who have made no such mistake. One example will do.

Culture Raising

There is a famous, centuries-old cry that gave root to modern democracy: *Vox Populi, Vox Dei* ("The voice of the people is the voice of God"). It's rooted in the Christian belief that as we are all made in the image of God, truth will eventually emerge from the authentically expressed voice of the people.

But radical Islamists, drawing strength from their own deep culture, believe there is no such thing, nor should there be. "Islam" means submission — to the truth. But only Allah knows the truth, and it was handed down to Muhammad who wrote it up in the Quran. This is a rigidly explicit, written truth without possibility of nuance or change. So forget your Charters and Bills of Rights. Only God has rights. Humans have duties. That's why, for committed Islamists, the democratic ideal is an outrageous blasphemy, and they have been, and remain quite willing, to die, if they must, to end it.

Democracy? When they are more numerous than us (wait for it), they will only need "one man, one vote ... once," to end democracy and govern by Islamic law.

France, which has had an obligation to take in millions of Arabs loyal to it since the disaster of the Algerian war, has an especially acute problem. The wearing of face-coverings in public has been prohibited in France since 2011. But Valérie Pécresse, head of the multicultural Île-de-France region surrounding Paris (which is now a no-go zone for French police, ambulances, and government officials

— and where you are unlikely to see a Muslim woman except in traditional garb), says[3] that Islamism "does not just have separatism as its objective," as French President Macron has said. "It has an objective of taking power."

The long-term strategy? They simply continue to have more babies than us, and to convert[4] thousands of our churches into mosques. Diversity? Only for multicultural suckers.

For the fundamentalist Muslims wandering around Paris, Toronto, or New York — so distinct from the ordinary nominal Muslims, content, even proud, to westernize or assimilate — conversion out of Islam for another faith is a capital offense. Death for the infidel. No pluralism there. These folks are not fooling around. I am not picking on Muslims. The fundamentalist Islamist variant just happens to be the deep culture in our midst doing the most aggressive rising.

Postnational State

How do we think all this gels with our patsy multiculturalism? It doesn't take a rocket scientist to see that the West has been busy dumping its own deep culture for the accommodating liberal pleasantries of its happy-face multicultural ideal. But some of the deep cultures now sharing our space — some of those more than 250 "visible minority communities" the government tells us are now rooted in Canada — are not necessarily following suit.

The Islamic enclave[5] of 260 homes in Vaughan, Ontario, for example, built exclusively for Ahmadi Muslims, is of interest. Ahmadis happen to believe in a post-Muhammad prophet named Ahmad, whom they worship. I happen to know a few Ahmadi who came to Canada from Pakistan where, like Christians and other "infidels," they were persecuted and many killed for blasphemy. I'm happy we have given them refuge. But the much larger question is this: After coming here, why have they banded together to take refuge from us in a Muslims-only home away from home on Canadian soil?

Historian David McCullough warned, "A nation that forgets its past can function no better than an individual with amnesia." And

---

3 See: https://www.theglobeandmail.com/opinion/article-macron-wages-a-war-on-islamist-separatism/

4 See: https://www.gatestoneinstitute.org/2761/converting-churches-into-mosques

5 See: https://immigrationwatchcanada.org/2007/10/06/giving-peace-a-chance-in-muslim-suburbia/

passive forgetting is bad enough. But active rejection? The lowering of one's own deep culture? That's another matter altogether, and I submit, a shameful one.

Just so, on Oct. 8, 1977, it was a distressing shock for patriotic Canadians to hear Prime Minister Pierre Trudeau declare to our House of Commons: "There are no official cultures in Canada." Well, the apple does not fall far from the tree. His son, Prime Minister Justin Trudeau told *The New York Times*[6] magazine in October 2015 that "there is no core identity, no mainstream in Canada," because "diversity is our strength[7]." But what about our unity? Oh well, Canada, he announced excitedly, is the world's "first postnational state." What?

Everyone knows that a state is a nation, and a nation is a state, don't they? So how can there be a "postnational" state? Then, I realized what he was saying. He was saying that you can ignore all the deep cultures on Earth, let them die a slow death, and live instead in what amounts to an "administrative state" with all the trappings of global bureaucracy (run by sweet folks like me).

A "postnational" state, he believes, does not need a particular "people," a "nation," or a "culture," to define it. It will be administratively defined as a multicultural, skin-deep holding-tank for … whoever wants to live there. It won't matter whoever. There will be no who any longer.

So in one sentence, Canada's self-satisfied, cheeky prime minister breezily dismissed two or three centuries of Canadian culture and history. Yet both father and son held forth knowing they have been direct personal and political beneficiaries of the West's deep culture as expressed and protected in their own … nation-state.

Beneficiaries, that is, of Canada's long struggle to create responsible democratic government, of our English Common Law and Parliamentary tradition, of the *habeas corpus* right, of an independent judicial system, of our long-cherished and defended system of private property rights, of ordered free-enterprise, and of the right to free speech (where even a PM can say things in public that are not true), and of so many more traditions of our uniquely Western way of life. Indeed, there has never been any other system that has reliably

---

6   See: https://www.nytimes.com/2015/12/13/magazine/trudeaus-canada-again.html

7   See; https://pm.gc.ca/en/news/speeches/2015/11/26/diversity-canadas-strength

produced such things. Nothing like it at all, nor, despite its faults, as good. Ever.

But Trudeau the Elder's statement was an archly clever move. He was determined to weaken the thrust of French separatism in Canada and the dominance of English culture at the same time by throwing both of them under the multicultural bus. Multicultural immigration would stabilize Quebec's falling population, weaken its French culture, dilute the separatist cause, and make the concept of "nation" meaningless. Eventually, who would care? He was confident that, eventually, all Canadians would be unified as skin-deepers to whom it would mean very little, to whom culture would soon be but a bauble or a trinket.

But there was immediate blowback. *Pur Laine* (pure wool) Québecers despised Trudeau's attack on their nationalist ambitions, and so have never promoted multiculturalism. Instead, Québec promotes "inter-culturalism," which is to say, "diversity" is tolerated there, but only as subservient to a dominant French nationalist framework defended by language and culture police who control the unquestioned supremacy of French and the unique deep culture of Quebec with draconian laws made necessary to fight off the threat of English cultural domination.

"To live in Quebec, is to live in French," is their motto.

So in effect, Canada officially dismisses its Anglophone deep culture to appease Quebec, while Quebec celebrates and defends its Francophone deep culture to dismiss Canada. Quebec is a proud bully culture fighting the Anglo multicultural diversity machine by standing its cultural ground. Anglos ought to do the same.

As mentioned, it was precisely because the various deep cultures of the world are so obviously not the same, and because many are legally, morally, and theologically incompatible, that the concept of self-defending nation-states was invented in the first place. So we can't go on pretending that blending them in a skin-deep mixture amounts to a real culture, for it doesn't, and it won't ever.

As I say, that clever but deeply false notion was invented by globalists to subdue patriotic national feeling in the West. And it has worked on the sleepy pretty well, producing deep-culture forgetting on a massive scale (ask any history teacher). But is it the best thing for Western civilization? I don't think so.

The antidote to forgetting is reminding. So leaving aside the easy litany of weaknesses and historical missteps, what will follow in my next article will be one man's unabashed effort to revive a deep culture awareness of at least a few of the glories of Western civilization. Maybe not the best deep culture possible — whatever that might mean. But on balance, one of the best the world has ever seen, and in many respects getting better all the time — which is why most of the immigrant traffic of the modern world is heading West, not East.•

Official White House portrait of President Donald J. Trump taken by Shealah Craighead on October 6, 2017 in Washington, D.C.

Source: Wikimedia Commons, public domain.

12. Beyond the Rhetoric: Trump Brings Back Founding Culture

NOVEMBER 8, 2019

A good friend amusingly described President Donald Trump as "the mouth that roared," attempting to define him as ineffectual. But he's the farthest thing from that.

In an age of slick television and internet imagery that has preempted the centrality of the spoken word, he's a startling throwback.

With words alone — in spontaneous off-the-cuff remarks, in unscripted speeches, and on Twitter — he's a fount of surprise. Sometimes he seems to surprise even himself, and could as well reply to a question: "How do I know what I think, until I see what I say?" That disturbs some listeners, but delights others.

But regardless, fans and foes alike the world over hang on his every word, and every word he thinks he said, or didn't say, as the world's media rise and fall in reaction to his moods, wondering what he will say or do next to shock their political sensibilities.

It all began with the stunned surprise of the career officers and experts complacently steering Steamship America to a more socialist destiny, when Trump singlehandedly crashed the control room, grabbed the wheel, and began turning the ship back from the brink toward which it had been heading — like every other Western democracy — for more than a century.

Taking the fractured social-engineers' shipwreck called America back to its original sovereign, free, nation-state foundation, is the underlying theme. Cut sprawling legislation, stop killing millions of unborn children, cut taxation, jack the economy, lower unemployment, get the poor off food stamps, kill the enemy then get out of foreign wars, fight for fair trade, control the nation's borders, become energy independent, disable outside agencies dictating domestic policy to America, and put judges in place who will defend the

Constitution as written. Back to the Founding! "America will never be a socialist country!" A busy man.

No public figure in recent memory has so brazenly and directly railed against the equality-mad, globalizing, anti-nationalist program that has been growing everywhere in the West like an invasive weed in the social and moral compost left by World War II.

Make no mistake. If the Cold War was World War III, we are currently in the thick of World War IV. It's a war against ourselves. Since 1648, when the Treaty of Westphalia halted the horrific wars of religion by institutionalizing specified rights of national sovereignty for the many different peoples of the world, there have been two incompatible conceptions afoot as to how we ought to live.

Globalism Versus Nationalism

Should each people, with a defined territory, ethnicity, language, culture, and political-economic system, evolve its own nation-state way of life, settling differences with other nations by way of agreements, treaties, and trade (as Westphalia wisely determined)?

Or should we be trying to unite all humanity under a single international system that defines the most rational political, economic, legal, and moral terms of living, thereby subordinating national ethno-cultural differences, in the hope of ending all wars?

These two ideologies — one nationalist, the other globalist — have been locking horns over mutually exclusive ends since Westphalia, like stubborn mastodons in a duel to the death, and they can never be reconciled. Tragically, during the last century, each of them embraced socialism — either national ethnic socialism (Germany and Italy), or international world socialism (all the communist countries) — as a means to further their clashing visions.

Although there are still remnants of each in our universities and on our streets, they were killed off as major forces in costly wars against the free world, against each other, and even against their own citizens — millions of whom were wantonly slaughtered as "internal enemies."

Then came the United Nations. At first, it was dedicated to peacekeeping, but since then, to the imposition of global moral, social, health, and economic standards on the world's nations by way of treaties aimed at regulating many of their internal affairs and sovereign rights.

Upon the heels of this came the European Union, weakening the national borders of European nations, unifying passports, currencies, and trade regulations under a single trans-national European standard. Diminishing the influence of any single national sovereignty or ethnicity over others was, and remains, its overarching agenda. No more power against power. The castration of national powers equally is the theme.

Such organized impositions on the sovereignty of nations are in effect a direct attack on the Westphalian international order, and Trump is the first leader in the free world to say loud and clear that he wants none of it. The rest of you can buckle to a global socialist-style bureaucracy if you want, but America? Never. We are going back to our unique national roots. MAGA: "Make America Great Again!"

But along with those efforts to dissolve tensions between nations has come a further effort to dissolve cultural hegemony within them, and the chief weapon as an effective solvent is the self-contradictory notion of "multiculturalism."

Multiculturalism

This term doesn't, as we may at first imagine, describe the adoption by a nation of many cultures. Rather, it's an attack on the very idea that any one culture is better — or has ever been better — than any other. If we declare all cultures to be equal in value, then none will have a right to dominance within any nation-state, is the theme.

That's how multicultural policy has become a weapon of cultural erasure — as was intended. Critics haven't been surprised to see that this has resulted in a lot of mini-nationalist enclaves within every Western democracy, complete with growing ethnic animosities, violence, and in some countries, even "no-go" zones where police dare not enter.

For as the prescient French critic Pascal Bruckner has said, multiculturalism condemns ethnicities to house-arrest in their own skins. So, let's see now … we fight nationalism between nations, only to create it a hundredfold within them?

Alas, these strategies for ending domination by a single national culture — the main target being the mostly Caucasian, Greco-Roman,

Judeo-Christian culture of Europe and North America, or what students used to call "Western Civ" — have been at work in all the democracies, fueled, as mentioned, by the justifying, though unproven assumption of the equality of cultures. So in the United States, the famous national melting pot — *e pluribus unum* (from many, one) — has been breaking down at warp speed into a salad bowl — *ex uno plures* (from one, many).

In 1988, in its own confused and self-contradictory campaign, Canada declared itself to be "the world's first multicultural nation."

Almost a decade prior to that, Canadian Prime Minister Pierre Trudeau had seen this policy as a novel means to dissolve the threat to Canadian unity posed by Quebec separatism, and to water down the dominant British cultural influence he disliked at the same time.

So he responded with characteristic flippancy to citizen complaints about this frontal attack on Canada's deep culture with a patently false statement: "It doesn't matter where the immigrants come from."

But he knew that it matters a great deal. That's why he was doing it. That's why he was keen to globalize Canada internally, so to speak, via mixed, nontraditional immigration.

The truth, however, is that Canada, just like the United States and most other nations descended from mother England, has always been "multi-ethnic," but never before "multicultural." What is the difference? It's quite simple.

Multiple ethnicities will assimilate under a single, deep culture they recognize as better than the one they left behind (that's why most of them came here), and will preserve their cultures of origin privately, if at all. But multiple cultures, if officially informed upon arrival that their culture of origin has equal value to the one for which they emigrated, will divide the population into as many cultures of origin as exist within the state. The former is a recipe for national unity; the latter for national disunity.

Canada has 20.6 percent foreign-born citizens[8], the highest percentage among the G8 nations. And while the federal government confirmed that Canada had "only six visible minority neighborhoods" in 1981, by 2001, there were 254, and who knows how many ethnic enclaves there are now? Census-identified foreign cultures

---

8   See: https://www12.statcan.gc.ca/nhs-enm/2011/as-sa/99-010-x/99-010-x2011001-eng.cfm

   BEYOND THE RHETORIC

now number more than 200 in Canada, and since 1980, far fewer immigrants have become naturalized Canadian citizens — a freefall from almost 93 percent naturalization[9] prior to 1981, to barely over 68 percent by 2010.

What ought to be worrisome is that so strongly do many immigrants now identify with their own cultures of origin that no one can be certain for whom they would choose to fight if Canada went to war with any of their countries of origin. They seem to prefer their own deep culture.

So what is a deep culture? It is to a people as a magnet is to iron filings. It attracts them. It pulls them toward itself and organizes their reality. If you scatter a few million iron filings on a table, they just lie where they fall in a messy jumble, pointing aimlessly like little arrows in all directions, at nothing in particular. However, the moment that you place a big magnet under the center of the table, all those aimless filings will immediately snap into line and point to the center, to the common pull of the big magnet. Big culture. Big magnet. A common attraction. *E pluribus unum.*

But take away the big magnet, and put 100 smaller magnets under the table instead, and what will you see? All the iron filings will reorganize, each aligning with the closest magnet. The nation-state is then de-centered. Little magnets. Little cultures. No common attraction. *Ex uno plures.*

Cultures can be deep. Very deep. They can also be skin-deep, moving around on the surface of national life without penetrating deeply into the national psyche. I don't want to dismiss the fun of skin-deep culture out of hand. Almost everyone living today has direct or indirect access to what has become an international skin-deep culture: French perfumes, bistros, and clothing; American movies; Japanese sushi restaurants; a passerby wearing a turban; lots of foreign cars buzzing around; and a congenial smattering of people with different colored skins and exotic features. Such things make high-consumption, chic societies more enjoyable. But they have no lasting pull. They are little magnets.

A deep culture is profoundly different. It's the big magnet of a common language, literature, religion, legal system, and economic

---

9   See: https://policyoptions.irpp.org/magazines/march-2018/what-the-census-tells-us-about-citizenship/

and political system that penetrates deep into the soul of the people in a thousand conscious and unconscious ways. Like that powerful big magnet, it draws citizens toward each other by way of shared cultural values, traditions, and principles, and most importantly, with the shared shalls and shall-nots of their common moral life. This is a natural product of the Westphalian principle, and it's currently under attack.

The problem is that citizens will willingly die defending their own deep culture, and throughout history have done so, in droves. But unless engaged in an alliance, they will seldom die for someone else's deep culture. Nor will they ever die for sushi, French perfume, or their sleek German car.

If you don't have citizens willing to die to defend your deep culture, you don't have a culture or a national home. You have a motel.•

A scene from the video created by The North Wire featuring William Gairdner.

Source: The North Wire, https://www.youtube.com/watch?v=bV5P3W_3OX4

13. The Four Stages of Liberalism

THIS video tells the story of how all the liberal democracies of the West have gone through four stages to get to where they are today.

I call the first stage "Virtue Liberalism," because the pursuit of virtue was the main interest of the Settlers and Pilgrims who came to the New World to escape the religious and social oppressions of the Old World. For them, liberalism was more about the "social freedom" they wanted to enjoy within their own communities than about their own individual freedom.

Most of all, they wanted to create a better world, to be free so they could be good. The idea of pursuing mainly their own personal pleasures and choices — especially those of a sexual nature — would have seemed extremely selfish to them, and possibly a sin.

Stage two may be called "Rights and Property Liberalism," because, by the middle of the eighteenth century, the ideas of the political philosopher John Locke were very much in the air, and they were displacing the former notion of social freedom. People were beginning to think of themselves more as free individuals living in states whose job it was to protect their natural rights and property.

Human slavery was a reality everywhere in the world at the same time, and in retrospect it was these powerful ideas about individual rights that eventually unlocked the door to civil rights for everyone in the West.

The key point is that it was a start-line philosophy: set the rules, run the race, and let the chips fall where they may. And it did a good job for a very long time.

But, by a century later, all the liberty-loving regimes of the Western world were slowly mutating into the equality-loving regimes we have today, which brings me to stage three, which I call "Equality Liberalism."

This mutation happened for a very simple reason: Liberty and rights were not producing the perfect society of which those first liberals had been dreaming.

At the end of the day, they saw that some were rich, some poor, some smart, some stupid, some hard-working, some lazy, and some, through no fault of their own, simply fell on hard times.

A permanent underclass was growing in their midst, and a shift was beginning from the idea of personal responsibility for one's condition in life to blaming "the system."

So the system had to be fixed. Equality would now have to be forced.

This meant the original start-line philosophy of liberty common to all the Western democracies was being replaced with a new finish-line philosophy of equality, and to ensure this, all of them were becoming "social democracies." But how can there be such a thing?

"Social" implies socialism, which mandates top-down control to achieve an equality of outcome for all.

But liberalism mandates a bottom-up freedom, with different outcomes as each might choose. A contradiction this deep would eventually mean policy paralysis and decline.

So it had to be resolved.

But the only way to keep the connection between the liberalism and the socialism would be to divide the body politic into two bodies: a private body and a public body, each with its own justifying will and ideology.

And this brings me to stage four, which I call "Libertarian-Socialism" — perfectly neither, but a fusion of both.

In order to fulfill the liberalism mandate, citizens would be allowed a lot more freedom for all things personal and private, especially those having to do with sex and the body, such as, contraception rights, abortion rights, easy divorce, homosexual rights, transgender rights, pornography rights, gay marriage, marijuana rights, euthanasia rights, and more — all made available in the name of personal choice, and many subsidized by the state.

As individuals, we, the people, have never been so open and free, would be the new branding.

But in order to fulfill the equality mandate, our once minimal governments had to begin an aggressive exercise of public will, to be funded by massively increased taxation and public debt, extending themselves into every conceivable aspect of national life.

The result is that libertarian-socialism is now a homogenized regime-type throughout the West, a political form so conducive to the growth of wrap-around government that many of these regimes have already become, what I call, "Tripartite States."

These are states in which one third of the people are makers, who produce the wealth; another third work for government at some level; and the last third are takers, who receive significant benefits in cash or kind from the state.

Anyone can see that in a democratic system the last two segments will always gang up on the first, like two wolves and a sheep voting on what to have for dinner.

This is now the sorry condition of the Western democracies: All citizens enjoy a maximum of bodily and sexual freedom, in the context of massive over-regulation, taxation, and control by the state of every other aspect of their lives.

And it's not going to change for the better, nor may we escape it, until citizens become far more conversant with the underlying ideological conditions that led us into it in the first place.

In order to shed light on those conditions, we all need to find out where we stand on the most important moral, social, and economic issues of our time.

Only then, can we begin the crucial discussions and debates with friends and neighbors that will make us a free and responsible people once again.•

Nineteenth-century painting by Philipp Foltz, depicting the Athenian politician Pericles delivering his famous funeral oration in front of the Assembly.

Source: Wikimedia Commons, public domain.

14. Democracy Against the Family

FOR more than a century, all of the modern democracies — each at a different rate — have been abandoning their foundation in ordered liberty for a new foundation of mandated equality.

This is justified as a necessary means to create a more fair and equal polity.

That has nothing to do with the original democratic promise of an equal start-line in the race of life, but, rather, with the creation by law of a more-or-less equal finish-line. Equal enough, that is, to garner more gratitude and thus more citizen-loyalty to the democratic state.

Ironically, this ambition is carried out by way of an incremental war on various kinds of privilege and moral distinction, created spontaneously by our own civil societies.

So the democracies are now at war with themselves. Privilege-producing civil societies, within equality-forcing democratic states, have ended up pitched against each other in a troubling battle to the death for citizen loyalty. Even though it's by far the more humanly gratifying, civil society is also by far the weaker, and has been losing the war badly.

One of the great ironies of our time is that we celebrate a public love of equality, but also of human community. But the latter can only be produced by a process of social-bonding that creates insiders and outsiders — or unequals. Let's see how that works.

Gaining Privilege

In order to pass from the status of autonomous individual to membership in a voluntary association, whether we are speaking of the Boy Scouts, a marriage, a religious group, a corporation, a charitable group, or a sports team — there are thousands of such groups — there will generally always be found (weak or strong, formal or informal) a solemn rite of passage to membership.

This is a four-stage process, the elements of which are *sacrifice, subordination, commitment,* and *privilege,* the last stage being the one that raises the panic and hackles of modern equality radicals.

Sacrifice refers to the moral requirement that individuals aspiring to join any social group must voluntarily agree to place the common will of the group above their own individual will, for all healthy civil associations are "we-based," rather than "me-based." This is also the most spiritual of the four elements, demanding a voluntary suppression of self. From this flows the bonding of group loyalty.

The motto of an organization such as Rotary International, for example, with its 35,000 member clubs and 1.2 million members, is "Service Above Self." If the willingness to sacrifice for other members is intentionally withheld, a member will usually be shunned, disinvited, or forced out.

Subordination refers to the requirement that for group discipline, all members must submit to the authority and rules of the group, without which no ruling hierarchy of authority is possible. Members carry an understanding, whether verbal or written, of the rules by which they feel bound and by which they proudly distinguish themselves from non-members.

Commitment is the public process whereby, the first two requirements having been met, a member will generally make a vow, or commitment, to the group, normally by way of an oath, a pledge, a written contract, or some simple signifying act bonding the member to shared group ideals and activities. The moment of this insider/outsider distinction between one citizen and an "other" is a profoundly anti-egalitarian moment — in today's terms, a profoundly anti-democratic moment — without which no human community can be formed.

Privilege is the reward stage, whereby specific benefits, privileges, and even protections are bestowed upon qualified members. This stage is usually accompanied by some kind of signifying ceremony in which the commitment or vow of loyalty is made, and by special symbols, costumes, handshakes, or celebrations intended to distinguish members from non-members. Sworn or signed-up members of innumerable civil associations are expected to be loyal, perhaps carry a membership card, wear a pin or a tie, be dutiful, pay dues, do any required work, abide by the rules, treat fellow members differently from — dare I say, better than — outsiders, and so on.

Most significantly, individuals who marry will sign covenants, wear rings, get lawful and exclusive sexual access to each other, and in societies that haven't completely capitulated to the egalitarian dispensation by extending heterosexual marital privileges to "any two persons" without regard to their procreative potentiality, will qualify along with their children for certain legal, tax, and social privileges until very recently only available to the union of one man and one woman.

Anyone can see that the human social-bonding process I describe is natural, preferential, intentionally exclusionary, and privileging. Always has been. But the modern democratic project is to weaken, circumvent, or destroy all hint of privilege that may embarrass the state's pledge to treat all citizens equally in terms of outcomes.

Needless to say, any fool knows that no two human beings are ever "equal" in themselves, and that naturally free and unequal human beings will very likely create naturally unequal outcomes. Hence, the attack by all the democracies on human social-bonding and the effort to convert it to state-bonding via the medium of forced equality.

Leveling Society

In the case of outright totalitarian systems such as communism and fascism, where the state's intent to dissolve, or at least hobble, civil society altogether is spelled out clearly in public policy, the attack comes from above. I hasten to mention that in the case of communism, this is an instructive irony, because Marx's theory predicted the "withering away of the state." But in every Marxist regime, the state has grown and thrived largely by absorbing civil society into itself. The gist of this essay is that we now see this very process at work in all the democracies, as well. On your Marx!

But in the case of the democracies, the attack on civil society tends to come not from above, but from within, by way of attacks launched by radicals who have drunk the state's equality Kool-Aid; this attack is less ideologically rigid, a little sloppy, but no less effective.

The result, in either case, is the radical disempowering, if not complete destruction, of civil society. I say "not complete," because that would be counter-productive. Egalitarian states that seek to engineer a swap of citizen loyalty from civil society to themselves are like the professional torture-master. They keep the victim weakened but alive as long as possible to get what they want, producing whatever goods the state may find essential and seek to control, but finds too difficult to create by itself.

Canada's single-payer health care system is a sterling example of this very tactic. A precise example of how the state's war against civil society is rolled out. The Canadian state regulates the quantity and kind of health care legally permitted throughout the nation, outlaws the private purchase or sale between citizens and physicians of all medical services controlled by the state, but relies on the tax-funded, state-controlled, and precisely limited reimbursement of private physicians, technicians, clinics, and hospitals to deliver it.

Of special interest is the manner in which many egalitarian objectives are achieved in the democracies, not by the dangerously unpopular idea of removing exclusive rights, privileges, laws, and protections from once-favored social groups such as the traditional family, but by boosting the tax base a little more and granting those same privileges and rights to every individual without the customary qualification (as mentioned, you just have to be one of "any two persons") and, in this fashion, removing formerly powerful distinctions that once conveyed exclusive social privilege, moral distinction, and status.

In effect, the democratic state eliminates various kinds of privilege by converting them into general welfare handouts. This has the same effect on once highly honored social institutions as giving a once-cherished medal for bravery to a coward.

The language of radical democracy at work in this demolition process is evident in our daily newspapers, if we care to see it. I keep a file of documents that has tracked this trend. The very first item is a Toronto Globe and Mail newspaper article of Nov. 25, 1999, describing how a lawyer, incensed that the legal and financial benefits of traditional marriage were at that time denied him, was determined to take his case all the way to the Supreme Court of Canada to argue that the law creates "sexual apartheid." Why? Because, he argued, it doesn't eliminate all social and moral distinctions between an almost infinite range of "family types."

His main point was that "*privileging* heterosexual relationships is contrary to the *equality guarantees*, and thus unconstitutional." He correctly landed on "privilege" and "equality" as the two opposing terms of the West's long civil war of values against itself that has been my focus here.

So we could say that in the name of equality, modern democracies are stealing customer loyalty from their own living societies, hoping for a more dead society and a more alive state. But this is a moral contradiction, since society is based on voluntary acceptance of membership and authority (it's morally alive) and the state on involuntary power (it's morally dead).

A New Terminology

What's to be done? We need to repudiate the state's self-serving centralizing language of egalitarian democracy in order to revive the social freedom and privilege-engendering authority that's a natural product of membership in all human voluntary associations. And that would mean inventing a new public terminology to de-emphasize forced equality as a democratic right, for the good reason that this claim operates mostly as a cover for more incursions of state power in its effort to transfer citizen loyalties to itself.

Be warned: When civil society is weakened to near-extinction, citizens lose their last buffer and protection against state power.

I'm imagining that such a language will respond to the call for more "individual rights" with a counter-call for "society's rights," and to a call for more personal "freedom of choice" with a counter-call for "social freedom" and hence, a strengthened (because normally bonded) "free society," rather than merely "free individuals." We need a public recognition that the privileging social-bonding process outlined above is absolutely essential for the formation of human community, that without human community there can be no civil society, and without a strong civil society, autonomous individuals are left naked before the power of the state.

Restoration of a more free society, then, would of course mean that individuals would be exposed to more, and more varied, forms of voluntary moral authority, with which they could deal as they wish — remain bonded to the group, or get out — but also to far less coercive power from the state. We would be more encumbered in terms of opportunities to fulfill the abundant moral obligations typical of all social-bonding, but less encumbered in terms of bending under raw power.

I think that would be a good deal. It would shift the ground of our political and moral relations from dependency on the grossly excessive ministrations and regulations of the state, to consent, independence, and belonging within real moral communities that serve as a buffer between ourselves and raw power. The point is that a return to a defense of the traditional rights and authorities of civil society can satisfy our longing for community, as well as for freedom within community.

Because most human beings long to belong, let it be together and by choice to the warm and privileging bonds of their own civil society, rather than alone and, by default, to the leveling state.•

THE idea that democracy, the political organization we know and love, might be incompatible with — or worse, might gradually be undermining — the most intimate human organization we know and love, called "the family," strikes most people as something close to heresy.

But is it?

When I presented this possibility to the World Congress of Families in Geneva in 1999, an awkward silence fell upon the room. No one moved or knew what to say. But 20 years later, I am persuaded more than ever of the Geneva argument, and I refresh it here for Epoch Times readers.

The Geneva Argument

Most of the disturbing changes in Western family life have to do with easily visible negative trends such as delayed marriage, falling birth rates, fatherless homes, poor single mothers, high divorce and abortion rates, and more. But research for my book "The War Against the Family" made it manifestly clear that, not far beneath the surface, there are invisible ideological forces rooted in the theory of democracy itself that are inimical to the formation and preservation of family life. That seems a little bizarre, so allow me to explain.

Every major modern democracy took root in the context of a protective faith culture where the good of all was foremost. They were "we" cultures in which the family was a near-sacramental institution rooted in privacy and freedom where natural human differences were expected to flourish. Equality before the law, and in the eyes of God, promised a fair starting line in the race of life, let the chips fall where they may. That was the dominant ideal, if not always met.

Accordingly, some families produced bright kids, some not so bright; some hard-working, some lazy; some rich, and some poor. As time passed, freedom and equality of opportunity produced a lot of successes. But a lot of distressing failures, too.

So the democracies of the West soon found themselves fretting over the possibility that by its very nature, a democracy will produce a permanent underclass. Freedom is not enough. Equality will have to be forced by the state. This meant the private family — proudly nourishing freedom, personal thriving, and natural differences — and the democratic state — nourishing forced equality — were on a collision course. They would be ideological enemies competing for citizen loyalty. Thus began the mutation of the Western democracies from their original equal start-line foundation to their present equal finish-line foundation.

It's no secret that throughout history, states that seek to grow by way of forced equality do so by regulating, controlling, and weakening — sometimes by outlawing entirely — the various subordinate powers and rights of the free social groupings that constitute their own civil societies. They don't want interference with the will of the state. Their objective — explicit in totalitarian systems, and subtly implicit in the softer forms of pervasive political regulation under which most of us now live — is to create a "national family" of equal citizens. Almost every national leader in the last century has used that expression.

The easiest way to understand how that is achieved is to think of the typical political ordering of a free people as having more to do with types of control than with degrees of freedom. Political reality may then be understood as a threefold structure:

1. At the top is the state, which relies on control of power and coercion through a monopoly of force exercised by law, police, courts,

jails, and weapons. All citizens of the modern world are members of coercive political states when born. There is no escape, for there is no stateless state.

2. In the middle is civil society made up of countless groupings we call free civil "associations" (and which Edmund Burke called "little platoons"), which rely for control not of power, but of moral authority and persuasion (from parents, employers, clergy, teachers, coaches, officers of organizations, and so on). We are members by birth in some of these associations, such as our family and our religious group, and others we choose to join or to leave at will. Other than for things illegal, the coercion of power is never part of the daily life of a free civil society.

3. At the bottom are millions of autonomous individuals who rely on self control. Historically, this is the milieu for religious faith, moral dualism (that familiar internal struggle between our personal angels and our devils), and the lifelong inner dialogue of freedom from, or slavery to, our own appetites and ambitions.

Moral authority, at least once we are adults, demands our consent as subjects and agents, while state power demands our surrender as political objects. The recent course of Western political history has been the attempt — overtly and very aggressively by totalitarian states, but covertly and more gently by democratic ones — to weaken if not wholly dissolve the traditional moral authorities and bonds of the middle layer of this political structure, leaving power at the top and, as the institution of the family in particular weakens, millions of increasingly autonomous individuals at the bottom. A bleak symbol of this baleful trend is the number of individuals now living alone — from 50 to 75 percent of the residents of many big cities of the West.

Atomization

The atomization of the social molecules of civil society in democratic states is achieved in two principal ways. First, by the state marketing the ideology of equal individual rights as prior in importance to the traditional privileging and exclusive social rights (and duties) of private civil associations. The primary target for any egalitarian is the destruction of privilege. But every civil association binds its member-ship with privileges. That's why democracy and civil society have been on a collision course for such a long time.

Secondly, the state atomizes by deciding to supply, or massively subsidize and market directly to, individuals at the bottom a myriad of actual goods and services that formerly were created by the free organizations of civil society. In the process, the state does an end-run around the middle layer altogether, thereby converting citizens from free moral agents and subjects beholden to each other to autonomous individuals who will now switch their allegiance to the state.

At this point, the free and equal start-line ideology with which we began may still get some lip-service as a historical ideal, but it's progressively smothered by the equal finish-line ideology that replaces it. This process is a work of strategic disorganization, an intentional disempowering and weakening of traditional society so that individuals dis-membered, so to speak, are by the same strategy exposed to the appealing order of rational state power as their newly dependable "family."

True conservatives (I use the terms "conservative" and "liberal" here in their historical and philosophical, rather than party sense) have always resisted this movement by preference for strengthening the traditional bonds of a free civil society (that is, free from an overly grasping state) and the natural obligations of moral, social, and family life that produce not liberty, but rather, ordered liberty. They will generally give priority to defending civil society (the "we" culture) over the wants of mere individuals (the "me" culture).

The key distinction is that the modern liberal-progressive goes in the opposite direction, making the claims of the autonomous indi-vidual (me) prior to those of civil society (we), and all the modern democracies have done this to different degrees and at different rates.

For those of us who saw the breakdown coming in Canada, the judicial war cry uttered by the late Chief Justice Antonio Lamer in 1992 — when he held forth, rather inelegantly during a newspaper interview — was ominous: "You know, I don't think society is an end in itself. I think a person is the most important thing. Anything else is there to assist the person to fulfill one's [sic] life … everything else is subordinate. Even collectivities." Atomization starts at the top.

In this respect, the modern liberal now believes the immediacy and free revocability of every personal choice — because it's sourced in personal will — is a mark of its sincerity and authenticity. That's why "choice" is today the mainstream mantra of democratic freedom, and the clearest signal pointing to the modern triumph of individual will even over biological nature (as so visible in the transgender movement).

The conservative, in contrast, takes the longer temporal view, concentrating on the binding power of human duty and obligation, even if this limits personal freedom and choice. And that's why G.K. Chesterton spoke of a "democracy of the dead," by which he meant that "the people" is rightly the whole civilization and moral tradition in which we are embedded, and not merely the heated gathering of the moment we happen to be in. It's why Burke defined civil society as a compact between the living, the dead, and those yet to be born. Real democracy is more about gratitude and obligation than personal will.

But the globalizing trend of what I have described elsewhere as "hyper-democracy" — whereby sovereignty, once deemed to reside in God, then royalty, then We the People, is now considered resident like some kind of secular soul in the autonomous individual — continues apace. One of the first and most striking — and strikingly absurd — examples of this tactic will do.

UN Egalitarianism

In 1994, the ambition to weaken the traditional family through the logic of egalitarian democracy was announced to the entire world by the General Assembly of the United Nations, which began a world-wide promotion[10] of "The International Year of the Family"

For a year and more, the U.N. threw its considerable battery of slogans, banners, and conferences behind the truly dumfounding idea that the family is "the smallest democracy at the heart of society."

Well now, that was pure drivel and bureaucratic meddling, because nowhere in the entire history of the world — except for a while by Plato, and then again for a while in the failed Kibbutz experiment of Israel — has the family ever been considered a democracy, nor should it be. I don't mean we shouldn't teach our children a wary respect for democratic ideals. But the family a democracy? Just try to

---

10   See: https://www.un.org/development/desa/dspd/international-year-of-the-family.html

imagine Mom and Dad with three or more children holding a vote on whether the children should attend school, or obey community moral standards, or be allowed to burp at the table, or — how subversive — whether Mom and Dad should have pocket money! Yet here was a bizarre, globalizing trumpet call from on high for the enforcement of the democratic "rights," "choice," and "freedom" of children. The subliminal theme was "the U.N. and 'democracy' will set you free."

But that could only mean the enforcement of children's rights as interpreted and supervised by government officials — usually against their own parents and their long-held family traditions. The civil societies of the West are presently having great difficulty — are actually ideologically quite disarmed — when it comes to resisting these statist intrusions, precisely because they are carried out in the radical language of a me-democracy that is our only political and moral language now, and we have not yet developed a higher pro-family, and pro-civil-society, language to fight back. This tells us we are in the presence of a political creed — or rather, of a political religion — that has reached an advanced stage of confusion.

As an example, I personally sat at a meeting of dignitaries, politicians, and social scientists in Calgary, Canada, addressed by one of the hundreds of emissaries who were being flown around the world by the U.N. during its Year of the Family to preach and avidly promote the idea that the family is a democracy. I listened with patient incredulity, then asked her how she would define "the family."

As if by rote, she quickly trotted out the idea that the family is "any group of people who associate with each other, work together, and care for and support each other."

So I asked her, "Would the 20 people in this room qualify?"

She paused for a second or two, hand on chin, as if thinking deeply.

And then said: "Yes. We should be called a family."

All jaws dropped at once.

Democracy, indeed.•

System Change, not Climate Change Demonstration in Vienna during COP21 in 2015. Activists forming the words system change.

Source: Wikimedia Commons, public domain.

15. Climate Change Confusion: What Are We to Think?

THE climate wars are an international disgrace. For a half-century, the public has suffered a bombardment of disputed facts about "anthropogenic global warming" (AGW) as well as so much undignified smearing of the work and reputations of skeptics by alarmists, and vice versa, that it's hard for anyone concerned about our beautiful planet to know what to think.

So I decided to look into the situation for myself.

I started by examining a temperature graph of a drill-core taken through deep sediments that make up the seafloor. And what did I see? Right before my eyes, were continuous, and sometimes extreme, climate fluctuations, from hot to cold and back again, non-stop, for two million years. Two million years! That was a shock. And it got me asking a lot of questions.

Is Earth Warming or Cooling?

The weak consensus — also disputed — seems to be that we've had both warming and cooling recently, and if we can be confident in climate measurements (which, as I shall suggest below, there is plenty of reason to doubt) we may, on balance, have warmed a little — less than 1 degree Celsius — during the last 100 years. Should we be alarmed by this, or impressed by the extraordinary stability of climate on a planet this size?

Half of that warming occurred between 1910 and 1940, prior to any serious fossil fuel emissions, and no climate model can explain the reason(s) for that. Then there was a cooling from 1950 to 1970 during the post-war industrial boom, just when (if the theory is correct) there ought to have been lots of AGW. After that, a report was issued by the U.S. National Academy of Sciences warning that "we may be approaching the end of a major interglacial cycle, with the approach of a full-blown 10,000-year ice age a real possibility," according to the March 1, 1975, issue of Science News. Then, we (maybe) had an unexplained no-change "hiatus" from about 1998 to 2013, even though CO_2 levels rose.

By now, like so many watching and wondering about all this, I'm feeling a little jerked around. And here's another reason: Prominent alarmist scientists of the Intergovernmental Panel on Climate Change (IPCC, a U.N.-sponsored agency) have been warning us for three decades that we are experiencing catastrophic global warming, with attendant sea-level rise, floods, fires, and hurricanes.

But there's energetic disagreement from a large group of prominent scientists, which can be seen in their report of 2016, "Why Scientists Disagree About Global Warming," published by the Nongovernmental International Panel on Climate Change (NIPCC).

Their argument is that any modern warming is natural and in line with historical variability; that increases in CO_2 have followed increases in temperature, not the reverse; that solar effects may be equal to or greater than effects of CO_2; and that a warming even of 2 degrees Celsius or more wouldn't be harmful.

What Is Future of the Planet?

No one knows the future. Climate scientists in the NIPCC report, above, tell us that "over recent geological time, Earth's temperature has fluctuated naturally between about 4 Celsius and minus 6 Celsius with respect to twentieth-century temperature." But we do know the past: The last 2 million years saw a pendulum-like oscillation between cold glacial periods of some 90,000 years each, with warm interglacial periods — we are nearing the end of one now — each lasting about 15,000 years.

For all that time, our planet was 90 percent cold, with brief stretches of warmth. A reasonable person might think we could use a little warming.

What Are Greenhouse Gases?

This term is used to create the impression that humans are massively fouling the atmosphere with carbon dioxide (CO_2) from the burning of fossil fuels that create a "greenhouse" on Earth, which traps heat that would otherwise escape into the upper atmosphere (which, confusingly, satellite reports tell us has been cooling recently).

But I was surprised to learn that Earth's greenhouse layer (without which we would sizzle to a cinder by day, and freeze solid by night), is quite natural, and is almost entirely created by natural water vapor and clouds. Of all atmospheric gases, CO_2 makes up only 0.04 percent, and anthropogenic CO_2 makes up only 3.4 percent of that figure: which is to say, 3.4 percent of 0.04 percent — a minuscule percentage.

When measured directly, the quantity of natural CO_2 on Earth is expressed in parts per million (ppm) of all atmospheric gases, and it has also fluctuated a lot. About the time of the Industrial Revolution, prior to any AGW, there were about 280 ppm, and it has climbed very slowly since then to about 410 ppm today, which is causing a lot of alarm.

But is that warranted? The lowest number found in the geological record is about 180 ppm, and during the Cambrian period — 550 million years ago — there were natural highs of more than 4,000 ppm, and higher. More confusing, however, is that there have been many long periods when temperature and the quantity of atmospheric CO_2 were unrelated (or "uncoupled"), and sometimes inversely related. Many argue that Earth is presently carbon-starved.

How Is Climate Measured?

The vast oceans, deserts, ice sheets, and mountain ranges of the Earth are reservoirs of heat and cold 196,900,000 square miles in extent. Despite best efforts to get good data — mainly from American, English, and Japanese sources, altogether monitoring thousands of sites — large parts of the Arctic, Antarctic, Brazil, Africa, Siberia, and the Earth's deserts are "data gaps." One example will do: In 2017, the World Bank reported that more than half of Africa's land-based stations, and 71 percent of its upper-air weather stations "do not report accurate data."

And the Northern Hemisphere — especially the United States — is far more extensively sampled than the Southern. So what do climatologists do? In a very nonscientific move, they average the temperature of the two hemispheres. It's a bit like saying that if the lower floor of your home is 18 C, and the upper floor is 24 C, your home has an average temperature of 21 C, when, in fact, none of it does.

A rather serious concern is that many decades ago, climatologists placed their thermometers outside urban areas. But most of those have been overtaken by urban "heat islands" that drive temperatures up unnaturally. So observations are "adjusted" to arrive at what scientists believe the temperature might have been without heat islands. But how could anyone be certain of something that wasn't measured?

As for NASA's reporting on climate? One insider (search for "NASA's inconvenient ruse"[11]) has reported thousands of pairs of "dummy" temperature records. And a German scientist has exposed[12] more fiddling with the climate record.

One of the first-ever studies[13] of an entire century of temperature readings reported that after adjustments for reading errors, omissions, and gaps, only 18.4 percent of Earth's surface had actually been covered by what was published as a "global" sampling.

Are Climate Models Accurate?

Climate predictions are developed via powerful computer programs called general circulation models (GCMs) that combine all sorts of inputs from land, air, oceans, and satellites. We know that a probability model can handle two variables like cloud change and wind change quite accurately. But when more are introduced, such as water vapor, solar radiation, absorption, and reflectivity from ice and cloud cover, well, the heart sinks at the probability of miscalculation and wobbly prediction.

Accordingly, all climate models have built-in "parameters" — adjustments for so-called "feedback" mechanisms, "forcings," and "flux tunings," to name just a few. What will happen if we double the estimate of CO_2? And so forth. But no one really knows, or could know. So at least one IPCC modeler has called such efforts "computer-aided story-telling." Others refer to it all as "synthetic data."

---

11 See: https://www.forbes.com/sites/larrybell/2011/07/19/nasas-inconvenient-ruse-the-goddard-institute-for-space-studies/?sh=5990118d6963

12 See: https://notrickszone.com/2015/11/20/german-professor-examines-nasa-giss-temperature-datasets-finds-they-have-been-massively-altered/

13 See: https://www.int-res.com/articles/cr1998/10/c010p027.pdf

As Earth's climate has never stopped fluctuating warm and cold, however, a reasonable question might be: Why do all climate forecasting models "run hot" instead of cold, or somewhere in between? At this point, any curious citizen would begin to suspect scientific bias and political motives.

What Is the Effect of Solar Brightness, Cosmic Radiation, and Orbital Wiggles?

Many skeptical scientists are convinced that the activity of the sun (along with other cosmic events) rather than the burning of fossil fuels, is the cause of the present warming, because the sun follows (on average) an 11-year cycle during which its brightness rises and falls according to changes in solar magnetism. Earth's surface temperature tracks those changes very closely.

The next dimming phase is supposed to occur around 2020. So, as if on cue, NASA[14] sent out a warning in October 2018 that we are entering what could be a long global-cooling period due to this natural fluctuation in solar brightness.

In addition to that cycle, every two centuries or so the sun's brightness level drops significantly during what is called a "Maunder Minimum[15]." The first ever noticed (by a fellow named Maunder) was from 1650 to 1710, during which Europe and North America went into a deep freeze, alpine glaciers extended over valley farmland, sea ice crept south from the Arctic, and Londoners played hockey on the River Thames.

Another observation that seems to support the solar thesis is that Mars, the only other planet to reveal its climate secrets, is right now coming out of an ice age without any AGW influences.

There are also the effects of planetary wiggles to consider. Our climate is affected by the changing shape of Earth's orbit around the sun from circular to elliptical over a 100,000-year period, by the wobble of its axis, and by the variance in equatorial and orbital planes. Taken all together, these complex motions of our planet correlate highly with ice ages on Earth.

---

14   See: https://thenewamerican.com/nasa-sees-climate-cooling-trend-thanks-to-low-sun-activity/

15   See: https://media.breitbart.com/media/2017/10/Holocene-Cooling-Iberian-Range-Tejedor-17-LIA.jpg

Will There Be Global Flooding if Ice Melts at the Poles?

Spoiler alert: Thanks to Archimedes, we know that anything floating in water such as the entire Arctic ice cap, displaces its own weight. So if the entire ice cap were to melt tomorrow, it would not raise sea level one bit. Only ice sitting on land that ends up in the ocean by calving from glaciers or by melting and running into the ocean will do that.

The average annual temperature in the high Arctic is about minus 34 C, and the coldest months range from minus 35 C to minus 50 C. It's a little hard for most people to fathom why a rise of less than 1 C averaged over the entire planet would change very much up there.

My own anecdotal evidence: Sixty-one years ago, in the summer of 1957, I worked as a cabin boy on a 10,000-ton tramp steamer delivering supplies to a couple of dozen permanent Cold War military and meteorology staff stationed at Resolute Bay in the high Arctic, about 1,000 miles from the North Pole. We arrived in open water on Aug. 18 and worked about two weeks in cool weather. In September 2018, the manager of a Canadian Arctic shipping company reported[16] that a cargo ship was delayed unloading at Resolute because "the thickness and concentration of ice is worse than we have ever seen since we started servicing the communities [in 2008]." Climate change, indeed.

Antarctica, on the other hand, where the ice cap sits on land, is the highest and coldest continent on Earth. It's more than 5.4 million square miles in extent with an average altitude more than 8,000 feet, has 2,660 mountains (one over 16,000 feet), and is covered with ice averaging more than 6,000 feet in thickness.

As for those massive ice sheets extending over water? The glaciological record shows there have been many retreats of the West Antarctic ice sheet that left it more than 100,000 square miles smaller than it is today. And we also know that the Eastern ice sheet has been cooling for the past half century. And really, a concerned citizen might want to know, how could a slight warming of Earth (if that is true) change much on such a massive continent where the average annual temperature is minus 50 C, and where, in 2013, the coldest temperature ever recorded on Earth was minus 93 C?

---

16   See: https://www.cbc.ca/news/canada/north/cargo-ship-ice-resolute-1.4812293

A Causal Connection Between Carbon Dioxide and Temperature Change?

What raises many serious questions about CO_2 and global warming is the shock of learning that there have been centuries-long periods when Earth was warmer[17] than today, such as the Minoan, Roman, and Medieval "non-greenhouse" warmings, in the complete absence of any anthropogenic CO_2.

Although we know the amount of CO_2 has been increasing since the Industrial Revolution, there is argument about cause and effect. Alarmists claim rising CO_2 (for which they blame industrialization) causes warming, while skeptics argue that historically, rises in CO_2 have followed, rather than preceded rises in global temperature, sometimes by hundreds of years.

To underscore this point, the NIPCC stated that "temperature and CO_2 are uncoupled through lengthy portions of the historical and geological records; therefore, CO_2 cannot be the primary forcing agent for most temperature changes."

How Do Plants Respond to CO_2 Enrichment?

Although CO_2 has a bad name, it is in fact a rich nutrient for all plant life on Earth, and without it this would be a dead planet.

Controlled experiments in which plants such as orange trees and wheat are force-fed CO_2 at high levels of enrichment as much as triple the plants' rates of growth. NASA satellite views show that our currently rising level of CO_2 is causing a greening[18] of the globe. There are arguments that by boosting crop yields, more CO_2 would be a boon to the poor worldwide.

How Much CO_2 Is Too Much?

In historical terms, concentrations of CO_2 have varied widely over geological time, with peaks 15 or 20 times higher than at present, and troughs just under half of today's level. In other words, current levels of this life-enhancing gas are very low. That's why prominent scientists, such as Princeton's Dr. William Happer, head of President

---

17   See: https://www.reddit.com/r/climate/comments/51ils7/greenland_gisp2_ice_core_last_10000_years/
18   See: https://www.nasa.gov/feature/goddard/2016/carbon-dioxide-fertilization-greening-earth

Donald Trump's recently formed Presidential Committee on Climate Security, argue that Earth is presently carbon-starved.

Amounts of carbon are measured in gigatons of carbon (Gt C), one gigaton being a billion metric tons. The annual production of carbon from fossil fuel emissions is estimated to be roughly 9.8 Gt C. Is that a lot? To understand its significance, we have to ask how much natural carbon there is on Earth today, where it is, and how much of it moves from place to place.

The Earth's atmosphere holds around 750 Gt C; the surface of oceans about 1,000 Gt C; the intermediate and deep oceans about 38,000 Gt C; and the Earth's natural vegetation cover and other surface matter about 2,200 Gt C. There is another 300 Gt C that moves around between oceans, air, vegetation, marine life, and ocean surfaces and depths, and so all known and estimated amounts are well over 40,000 Gt C.

Is There An Agenda?

It seems increasingly apparent that the science of climate has all but wholly mutated into the politics of climate. Accordingly, we are getting more and more scare-statements warning that AGW is going to bring the world to an end within 12 years.

Below is a sampling of those fears and calls to revolution, of which the "Green New Deal" is just the most recent. This article (and the questions it raises) is offered as an antidote to those fears.

- **Dr. Judith Curry[19], formerly of Georgia Institute of Technology, 2019:**
  "Climatology has become a political party with totalitarian tendencies … [it is] becoming an increasingly dubious science, serving a political project … the policy cart is leading the scientific horse."

- **Maurice Strong[20], who organized the first U.N. Earth Climate Summit (1992) in Rio de Janeiro, Brazil:**

---

19   See: https://www.forbes.com/sites/larrybell/2013/01/22/the-u-n-s-global-warming-war-on-capitalism-an-important-history-lesson-2/?sh=11683a4829be

20   See: https://www.forbes.com/sites/larrybell/2013/01/22/the-u-n-s-global-warming-war-on-capitalism-an-important-history-lesson-2/?sh=11683a4829be

"We may get to the point where the only way of saving the world will be for industrialized civilization to collapse. Isn't it our responsibility to bring this about?"

- **IPCC official Ottmar Edenhofer,[21] November 2010:**
  "… one has to free oneself from the illusion that international climate policy is environmental policy. Instead, climate change policy is about how we redistribute de facto the world's wealth …"

- **Christiana Figueres[22], executive secretary of the U.N.'s Framework Convention on Climate Change, 2019:**
  "This is probably the most difficult task we have ever given ourselves: to intentionally transform the economic development model for the first time in human history."

- **Rep. Alexandria Ocasio-Cortez[23] (D-N.Y.), February 2019:**
  "This is really about providing justice for communities … So, really the heart of the Green New Deal is about social justice."•

---

21 See: https://www.dailysignal.com/2010/11/19/climate-talks-or-wealth-redistribution-talks/

22 See: https://sovereignnations.com/2019/02/07/global-warming-destroying-capitalism/

23 See: https://thehill.com/policy/energy-environment/428902-ocasio-cortez-unveils-green-new-deal-climate-bill/

Lobby card for the American drama film *Men and Women* (1925).

Source: Wikipedia, Paramount Pictures, public domain.

16. Sex Differences, and the War Between Nature and Nurture

MARCH 14, 2019

"**G**IRLS AND BOYS are as different from the neck up as they are from the neck down."

> — Psychologist and author JoAnn Deak, in her speech
> *"Taking the Mean Out of Teen"*

For more than 50 years, the standard social-science model has insisted that differences between the sexes — and therefore their different social outcomes — are learned from the environment (from nurture). But over the same period, science has revealed a large number of measurable sex differences that are rooted in the structure and function of the brain, and in biology (in nature).

Most Western democracies began as nature societies. They believed that both sexes would express their natural biological differences in the personal choices and outcomes of their lives. This kind of society calls for liberty and the free expression of natural differences under a rule of law that is the same for all.

But those same democracies slowly mutated into nurture societies, resting on the belief that all human beings are the same and, therefore, their differences must be socially constructed. Accordingly, they call for a regulatory war against all sorts of inequalities, and for differential laws imposing discriminatory policies against some groups of citizens in favor of others.

By providing fact-based evidence that a great many differences between the sexes are natural and hard-wired, however, scientists armed with high-tech machinery have been steering us into a renewed ideological war between nurture and nature, and therefore into a clash with our own public philosophy. The outcome of this war between hard-science nature and soft-science nurture is going to be interesting.

In no particular order, here is a brief overview of some measurable natural sex differences, all of which can be easily found by searching the internet for scientific papers on cognitive sex differences, male versus female sex differences, the psychology of sex differences, and so on.

Gendered Senses

Even while still in the womb, male and female babies behave differently, and moments after birth, they show different interests and intensities of reaction to the same objects, sounds, and tactile sensations.

As newborns, girls are more sensitive to sounds, smells, tastes, touch, voice, and musical nuances than boys. A girl's sense of smell is anywhere from 200 to 1,000 times keener than a boy's; sense of touch, twice as sensitive; and sense of hearing, two to four times keener than a boy's. The eyes of baby girls are far more sensitive to the long-wavelength light spectrum than those of boys, and they can detect much lower concentrations of sweet, sour, bitter, and salty tastes than boys can, and have quite different taste preferences almost from birth.

A Baby's Cry

This seems rather telling: Infant girls — but not infant boys — will easily distinguish a baby's cry from other general sounds.

Boys and Objects

Although baby boys get as much affection and physical contact from their mothers as do girls, they nevertheless tend to prefer objects to people.

Girls and Language

All researchers report that girls tend to develop and process language, language fluency, and verbal memory earlier than do boys.

Play Differences

Girls are less rule-bound, while boys are more so. Boys want rules telling them if they are winning or not, so they generally prefer rank-related play — a difference seen later in work as well as in play. Boys more vigorously seek play rewards, such as stars, medals, beads, win-or-lose titles, and so on. This is especially visible in materialistic societies. Hence, the amusing but rather sad quip: "The man who wins in life is the one who dies with the most toys."

Human Cognitive Patterns

In "Sex and Cognition," an impressive survey of male/female differences, behavioral psychologist Doreen Kimura concluded that "human cognitive patterns and their related brain organization are permanently influenced by physiological events [mostly hormonal differences] that take place by the fourth fetal month." I should add that plenty of research shows that opposite-sex traits can be induced in males and females via hormones.

Boys and Girls Have Different Brains

Evolutionary psychologist Steven Pinker, in "The Blank Slate: The Modern Denial of Human Nature," performed a definitive take-down of the centuries-old theory that the human brain begins life empty, so to speak — like a blackboard or slate with nothing written on it — and then is slowly made operational by physical stimuli and social conditioning. Not entirely so. Modern scanners have found that the physical brains of boys and girls are different in many fine details, especially from puberty onward.

Brain Metabolism

At the University of Pennsylvania School of Medicine, a combination of positron emission tomography (PET) scans and high-resolution magnetic resonance imaging (MRI) technology was used to study brain metabolism and showed that even while at rest, males and females differed in 17 areas of brain function.

Males and Violence

At puberty and through young adulthood (15–25 years of age), men are far more prone to physical violence and women more prone to emotional volatility. With age, men tend to become less aggressive (due to falling testosterone levels) and women more aggressive (due to falling estrogen levels). Researcher Glenn Wilson, in his very readable work "The Great Sex Divide: A Study of Male–Female Differences," reported that about 85 percent of all crimes of aggression are committed by males, and there are specific, universal sex differences in the crime styles, types of victims, and post-crime behaviors of male and female perpetrators of violent crimes.

Spatial Skills

Research also shows boys are better than girls at a variety of spatial skills, such as mentally rotating a drawing of an object (called "imaginal rotation"), including 3-D rotation. This skill is cross-cultural and "practically universal" in males. This spatial skill sex difference becomes quite marked after puberty in humans, and is a sex difference also observed in animals.

Location of Objects

Women are superior to men at certain tasks requiring memory for the location of objects. This is especially evident during self-location in space: Women tend to do poorly at map-reading compared to men, opting instead to locate their position by memory of objects and landmarks ("turn left at the coffee shop"). Men, in contrast, tend to think in terms of compass directions ("turn north when you get to the corner"). Removing landmarks handicaps women, while changing dimensions handicaps men.

The Aggression Difference

From birth, boys are more aggressive, competitive, and self-assertive than girls, and this is the most common finding, worldwide. Interest in this difference became mainstream in 1978 when professors Eleanor Maccoby and Carol Jacklin of Stanford University, both doctrinaire feminists hoping to find proof that there are no innate sex differences, "sifted the evidence" and simply surrendered. Their landmark publication, "The Psychology of Sex Differences," offered a mass of evidence that the higher aggression of boys is innate and can't be attributed to social construction.

I'm not sure why we needed social scientists to tell us this, as everyone knows that boys the world over are punished far more severely and frequently than girls for aggression, and nevertheless remain far more aggressive. And as one observer put it: Anyone who has raised both boys and girls and still thinks they are the same has already withstood far more evidence to the contrary than any social scientist could ever provide.

My addendum to this is that aggressiveness and control are very different. Just because men are generally more aggressive doesn't mean they always end up with control. Everyone can think of couples where the male is more aggressive, but the female controls the relationship and the tenor of the family. I remember a great line from the movie "My Big Fat Greek Wedding."

The mother says to her daughter: "The man is the head of the family. But the woman is the neck. And she can turn the head any way she wants."

An amusing and deep truth.•

Sixteen years of BC Liberal neglect and underfunding has created a crisis in public health care. An estimated 30,000 people in Kamloops are without a doctor. Overcrowding is the norm in emergency rooms, hospital hallways, and at walk-in clinics where families line the block waiting to see a doctor.

Source: Wikimedia Commons, public domain.

17. So Americans Want Canadian Health Care? Think Again!

FEBRUARY 11, 2019

AT the end of January, a rather smugly proud Gov. Gavin Newsom of California and a feisty Mayor Bill de Blasio of New York appeared on U.S. national news on the same night, the former to announce free "guaranteed health care for all Californians" and the latter, free "universal health care" to all New Yorkers.

The United States is talking about trying Canadian-style socialized medicine.

I've been a fairly contented user of Canadian socialized medicine my entire adult life, and I know a lot of good people in the system. But I'm also a public critic of it, due to its expense, delays, and limitations, but especially because there's simply no moral justification for the forced socialization and policing of health care in a free society.

Ideologically speaking, no socialized medicine scheme can succeed for long, because the very principles and deceptions by which it is justified lead to its downfall. Canadian socialized medicine is near the end of a long process of consuming itself both ideologically and financially. So, in what follows, I offer a few warnings to our U.S. friends.

Lies About 'Free' Health 'Insurance'

When it comes to government-controlled, single-payer health care, the word "free" is an illusion. So is the word "insurance." Nothing is free — although it may be prepaid for you by someone else. The province of Ontario, where I live, has an "Ontario Health Insurance Plan" (OHIP). It's a well-meaning Ponzi, or "pay-go," scheme, as economists say, because there is no insurance, and never has been. Money is simply taxed from mostly younger working people and doled out for the health care of mostly older sick people. In Ontario, 10 percent of the citizenry (mostly seniors) consumes 77 percent of all health care.

Socialized Medicine Is Very Expensive

Canada's state-controlled system is per capita among the most expensive in the world ($6,839 for every citizen in 2018). But it rarely gets a B from international agencies ranking national health care systems. A 2017 Commonwealth Fund study of 72 metrics of health care in 11 nations ranked Canada third from the bottom. The United States ranked last, which is an irony, because the United States has the best medicine and medical science in the world, but not the best medical delivery system.

A further irony, when comparing medical spending, is that there is no particular connection between national health care spending and the health of citizens. Many countries, such as Japan, spend as little as half of what Canada spends (and a third of what the United States spends), but their citizens are no less healthy, and often more so.

Canada and the United States each spend about 7 percent of GDP on public health care. The rest of Canada's roughly 11 percent total, and the United States' 17 percent total, is private. Canada's program is publicly administered, but privately delivered under strict state controls. The difference in the totals is because American citizens are still free to spend as much of their own money as they wish on additional private health care and insurance, whereas Canadians aren't. Individual doctors and medical institutions in many provinces of Canada are subject to prosecution and serious fines for providing private care in competition with the public system. You could say Canadians are health care prisoners.

Canada's Experience

Canada formalized its socialized health care program with the Canada Health Care Act of 1984, which insisted on provincial compliance with certain "principles" of the Act, such as universality and accessibility. The federal government then offered massive cost-sharing subsidies — a form of fiscal bribery — to all provinces in exchange for coast-to-coast compliance with the principles. Provinces found in breach have been docked millions of dollars.

The act made Canada, along with North Korea and Cuba, one of the few countries in the history of the world to outlaw private medical care (though North Korea and Cuba have recently dropped the ban). Ontario can issue fines of up to $25,000 to individuals and hospitals found guilty of queue-jumping (although, as I shall point out, there is lots of that). This calls for a lot of inspectors and surveillance.

Medical Police

Canada's once-free physicians soon realized their entire profession was going to be overseen by — there's no other word for it — medical police. There would be strict state control and scrutiny of fees, fines for contraventions of the act, and queries from government inspectors about the "reasonableness" of additional treatments or referrals to specialists.

My own general practitioner (GP), a good and caring man, has remarked to me often, when I inquire about possibly being allowed a certain additional treatment, "Well, I don't suppose that would be an abuse of the system." He means that, in my case, he's decided that it's justifiable to spend scarce public money on me (and that he'll be able to defend his decision if questioned by the medical police). So you see, he's not just my doctor. He's my medical master and gatekeeper.

eSnooping

All physicians in Canada used to swear on the Hippocratic Oath to maintain strict physician–patient confidentiality. But administratively speaking, that has evaporated. Poof! From the start of Canada's socialized system, any citizen's private medical file could be seized and reviewed by a medical officer of the state — perhaps your neighbor down the street? They have the right to open your file and inspect the private details of your reflux, your cancer, your hemorrhoids, your gall-bladder surgery, your erectile dysfunction, whatever.

But it gets worse. Now we have eSnooping. With recently updated electronic patient-record systems, health inspectors can now do all their peeking into your once-private medical history electronically. To reflect a little on such unlimited invasion of intimate privacy by a government official is to feel a slow burn.

Canary in the Mine

Canada is the canary in the mine for the United States' socialized medical future. So here's what can be expected. Socialized medicine is in competition for public funding with all other government services, such as roads, education, culture, policing, and so on. When it began in Ontario in 1968, the OHIP program accounted for about 25 percent of all expenditures.

There were lots of warnings from skeptics that triage of patients and rationing of scarce resources would soon begin, and government would be unable to control spending due to unlimited demand from patients and gaming of the system by doctors, nurses, specialists, technicians, medical equipment suppliers, and drug companies. And because Canada had turned the illusory notion of free medical care into a sacred "right," no one would dare limit it. Whenever they try, as a former premier of Alberta soon found out, "everyone's hair lights on fire."

Crowding Out in Socialized Medicine

By 2017, the cost for socialized medicine in Ontario had risen to 44 percent of all government expenditures, and it's heading straight for 50 percent. In a disturbing report on health care spending issued in 2012, Don Drummond, chief economist of the Toronto-Dominion Bank, warned, "Things will only get worse as health care eats up every other public service, like an insatiable Pac Man," and that it would rise to 80 percent by 2030.

Critics thought he was exaggerating. But in terms of a province's "own-source revenue" (total revenue, minus federal subsidies and debt repayment), many provinces of Canada are already very close to spending 80 percent of their own revenue on health care. As U.S. political satirist P.J. O'Rourke warned long ago: "If you think health care is expensive now, just wait 'til it's 'free!' "

Long Waits

Dr. Brian Day, a former president of the Canadian Medical Association, warned in a New York Times interview in 2006 that "[Canada] is a country in which dogs can get a hip replacement in under a week and in which humans can wait two or three years."

Vancouver's Fraser Institute, a highly respected think tank, published an annual survey of 12 medical specialties in 2018. It revealed that, on average, specialist physicians report a median wait time for medically necessary treatments of 19.8 weeks from referral by a GP to receipt of treatment.

The wait from first consultation to orthopedic surgery is the longest, at 39 weeks — 10 months — and from diagnosis to the start of oncology treatment, 3.8 weeks. For scans, it's 4.3 weeks for a CT scan, 10.6 weeks for an MRI scan, and 3.9 weeks for an ordinary ultrasound. The institute reports that, typically, more than a million Canadians are wait-listed for medically necessary treatments.

Waiting for care is so common that, in 2005, Canada's own Supreme Court publicly warned the nation that "access to a wait list is not the same as access to health care," and that in some serious cases — which are on the record — "patients die as a result of waiting for public health care." Citizens die because the government makes them wait for health care. What kind of country admits such a thing without shame and blushing? Toronto's mayor describes the sad spectacle of patients languishing in the corridors of overcrowded hospitals, as "hallway medicine."

A Multi-Tiered System

Socialized medical systems are never single-tier, as promised, or even two-tiered (that publicly dreaded possibility). They are, in fact, and inevitably, multi-tiered. First, there are several triage tiers — tiers within tiers — where patients wait differing lengths of time, according to the severity of their illness.

Then, there are the professionals, or even ordinary citizens, who just happen to know someone working in the system — the big-name athletes; the big business people; the media stars; the politicians; the police; the military brass; and, not surprisingly, doctors and nurses themselves, who get immediate care from their own hospitals. Finally, there's anyone who lives close to the best hospitals and doctors rather than hundreds of miles away. Unionized workmen get treatment for injuries in a week because the government doesn't want to get stuck with their disability payments, while an ordinary citizen may have to wait for months.

When I first began investigating the questions of medical tiers in

Canada, I discovered that many of Canada's members of Parliament in Ottawa were walking down the street for same-day medical care at a military hospital intended for soldiers only. That was halted once the story broke. And I almost forgot: Statistics Canada reports a huge tier of almost 2 million Canadian citizens who complain they have no doctor because Canada is short on doctors.

Medical Tourism Booming

There's another very large Canadian tier engaged in medical tourism. Thousands of Canadians — 64,000 in 2018 that we know of, and surely thousands more who aren't telling — travel a long way to countries such as the United States, Costa Rica, the Cayman Islands, Cuba, and South Africa for services that are unavailable in Canada. People in this tier spend close to a billion dollars per year in other countries, either because they are forbidden to spend it for private care in Canada, or because the services, technology, or specialists are not available here, or the pain and the wait are just too long.

Most shocking of all is that many of the people engaged in these expensive medical jaunts are the very politicians who write laws forbidding Canadians to spend their own money on private medical treatment. Among them are two former prime ministers of Canada (Joe Clark and Jean Chretien), two provincial premiers (Danny Williams and Robert Bourassa), and we suspect other government ministers and elected officials who aren't telling. These people want private health care for themselves, but not for the voters.

Private Clinics

Most of Canada's provinces have below-the-radar private clinics that operate in contravention of the Canada Health Act. Medical police pursue them for years to shut them down. Lawsuits follow. Some are shut down. New ones open up. More medical police. And around it goes.

The same Dr. Brian Day mentioned above has already spent $2 million in court fighting for the survival of his private medical clinic in Vancouver. Even though, when citizens pay his clinic for care, it reduces the government's expenditures, the government is trying to shut him down for ideological reasons. They argue that money in your pocket shouldn't determine the quality of care you get, even though the same government doesn't mind if money in your pocket determines the kind of condo, or car, or bicycle, or food you buy. And they go silent when informed that there would be a lot more money in everyone's pockets if the government weren't taking so much of it in the first place.

The most recent private initiative in Canada was to open private hospitals on Indian reserves, where Canada's laws against private medicine don't apply. Health Canada reacted sharply: Such private hospitals might be allowed, but only if they cater solely to foreigners.

Foreigners Can Pay Cash for Care

If you're a foreigner, and have cash — money from outside Canada's socialized system — immediate health care is available to you for, say, a surgical procedure today, for which a tax-paying Canadian may have to wait a very long time. So let's see now: A full citizen who has been paying taxes for an entire working life for medical care is forbidden by law to use personal funds to purchase the same surgery offered today to a foreigner for cash? That seems very wrong.

Physicians Gaming the System

And, of course, many physicians learn to game the system to keep their earnings up. Good, honest folk, for sure. But only human. Lots of studies have revealed that in any government-controlled health system with scarce resources, physicians may be found engaging in "time shuffling," "upgrading," "injury enlargement," "ping-ponging," "service splitting," "phantom treatment," "assembly-line treatment," and more. I didn't invent these terms. They are easy to find in the fevered calculations of health economists.

Veterinary Medicine for Humans

Surely, the most damning moral fact about any socialized medical system, however, is that it converts human medicine into veterinary medicine for humans. Think about it. The machinery, medicines, and procedures used to treat your pet dog or cat are the same as those used to treat you.

In a free and open society, humans have a say as to how much and what kind of treatment they want to purchase, or to insure themselves for, or to refuse. But animals don't: Animals have medical masters. Meanwhile, in a closed society with a socialized medical regime, the quality, availability, and timing of medical services that citizens are permitted to receive are dictated by their master, the state. It follows that socialized medicine is veterinary medicine for humans.

Is this what Americans want? •

Pro-Life demonstration in Washington.

Source: Wikimedia Commons, contribuator FamilyMan88, public domain.

18. Democracy, Abortion, and Slavery

"**A**LL who support slavery are free, and all who support abortion are alive."

The Legislature of New York State, in a burst of joyful freedom-talk, has just passed a law making late-term abortions (after 24 weeks) far more likely. It is not easy to get a live baby that age out of a pregnant mother's unripe womb, and most citizens are simply unaware of how that is done. In a future piece, I will explain some of the graphic realities and the moral and philosophical confusions relied upon to justify them.

But for now, there is a deeper layer that needs focus. All women understand that the work of childbearing and nurturing falls disproportionately on them, and so no democracy can "equalize" the sexes unless this natural biological inequality is somehow transformed into a chosen consequence of a woman's will.

Laws permitting abortion-on-demand achieve this result by enabling women to eliminate their unwanted children, leaving them only with wanted children, thus removing any grounds for complaint about unchoseninequality.

What this distinction tells us is that almost all modern democracies locate their moral justification for abortion in the will of the woman, and not in her biology. In this sense, all modern abortion regimes are an expression of the modern triumph of the will over nature.

Equal Freedom

In the past, the triumph over nature was achieved by careful women prior to the sex act — in which they denied themselves by an act of will, or via contraception — rather than by an act of will after the sex act. The will to sustain one's freedom formerly exerted before pregnancy has been transformed into control over the life or death of the unborn child in order to sustain one's freedom after pregnancy.

Presto — a woman can choose a freedom equal to that of any man, provided she is willing to kill her own child in the womb.

In most democracies, citizens are warned sternly on wine bottles and cigarette packages not to drink or smoke, for fear of "harming the fetus," but they may kill their own unborn child with impunity at any time prior to the moment of natural birth and drop it in the garbage. In Canada, which has no law against abortion whatsoever, this is a woman's right even up to the moment before natural birth.

Although I was once in favor of abortion for hard cases (though never as a general or contraceptive right), the facts of this grisly reality and what I believe is the inescapable logic of the arguments against it, have convinced me that abortion as practiced in all modern democracies must be judged a distinct moral evil no different in character from the early programs of death-by-infanticide practiced by the Nazi regime in Germany, and the genocidal programs engaged in by all other totalitarian regimes. They all engage in moral and legal trickery to make this possible.

Non-human

The common legal trick that enables them to kill human life in the womb with impunity is the same everywhere.

They invent a kind of category law to redefine the unborn child as a non-person or as not yet a human being, until "it has completely proceeded, in a living state, from the body of its mother" (this, from Section 223 of Canada's Criminal Code). This is often called the "born alive" rule.

The point is, the unborn human child is legally defined away as non-human prior to birth. Then you can do with it whatever you want.

Now, it so happens this was the same legal trick used by all former slave-owning regimes in history. They legally defined those they wanted to enslave as property, or chattels, or non-persons who could then be bought, sold, or killed at will.

All democracies that permit abortion are using the same trick. And that's why I say that almost all the modern democracies have become slave regimes of a new kind in which, in order to make women as free from biology as men, they have enslaved all unborn children.

What this is telling us is that, in order to resolve the contradiction at the heart of egalitarian democracy — the fact that we trumpet "equal freedoms and rights," even though men and women can obviously never be equals in natural biological terms — we have had to sacrifice a whole class of human beings by defining them as slaves.

In effect, in order to sustain the ideological purity of our democratic system, we have replaced chattel slavery with womb slavery, and all the modern egalitarian democracies that have done this have mutated into slave regimes of a new kind.

Slave Regimes

In ancient times, in places like Greece and Rome, millions of human beings outside the womb were made chattel slaves to sustain a political ideology resting on victory in war, disdain by the educated for manual labor, to ensure leisure for the practice of the democratic rights of citizens (only), and so on. In other words, chattel slavery was a political and ideological necessity for the preservation of the political philosophy of the nation.

In the totalitarian regimes of Adolf Hitler and Josef Stalin, the sacrifices to the system, so to speak, were all those defined and enslaved as "internal enemies" (Jews, ordinary liberal and conservative protesters, artists, and so on) whose very existence threatened the ideological purity of the state.

Until very recently, the classical liberal democracies of the West welcomed the full expression of human biological differences. They rested on an original foundation of individual liberty and the natural differences this produces. They professed an equal start-line philosophy that celebrated merit and opportunity, let the chips fall where they may. And we still give this lip-service, at least.

But in a mere half-century, most democracies have mutated from their foundation in liberty to a new foundation of mandated equality, which is an equal finish-line philosophy. This is now the dominant justification for our democracies, and it has produced a dominant contradiction: The democracies of the West simply cannot figure out how to realize their latest ideological promise to half of the citizenry without allowing the killing of unborn children. •

Saint Augustine by Philippe de Champaigne.

Source: Wikimedia Commons, public domain.

19. Augustine's Good and Evil

WHAT are we to think of a man who tells God, "I defied you, even so far as to relish the thought of lust, and to gratify it, too — within the walls of your church, during the celebration of your mysteries"?

He was a daring, in-your-face iconoclast. A wild fornicator, he had many mistresses and a bastard son. A self-confessed thief who declared "the evil in me was foul, but I loved it." How's that for modern liberation?

Those words were written in A.D. 398 by the man who became Saint Augustine, one of the fullest sinners and greatest saints in all Christendom, in his "Confessions," a book that is a joy to read, and read again, especially during the Christmas holiday season.

So I opened it recently and the thought arose that the power and the beauty of Augustine's physical and spiritual struggles are still, in microcosm, the ongoing and unsettled struggles of our anti-spiritual time.

In the churches of our secular lands, we see mostly sparse congregations, gray hair, and lots of women. Our spiritually hungry youth, seeking fire, discover mostly boredom and ashes there. And yet, the greatest surprise in reading Augustine isn't preachiness, not scolding analysis, but fire — his overwhelming passion and his burning emotional, sensual, and intellectual fervor.

His struggles centered on three main problems: the flesh, good and evil, and the cosmos.

As a youth, he traveled to Carthage to study, where, he writes, "I found myself in the midst of a hissing cauldron of lust." Sounds like a modern university.

There, he says, he twisted in the chains of pleasure, and loved "wallowing in filth and scratching the itching sore of lust." But he soon felt submerged by pleasure, locked in a mortal struggle with his own appetites, beyond which he saw nothing. So, one day, he cried out half-hearted for relief, begging God, "Give me chastity and continence — but not yet." He was still a young dealmaker.

And where are we today, but drowning in sensuality, submerged in it as a people. Our gigantic shopping malls post 50-foot posters of near-naked, voluptuous women leering seductively above throngs of shoppers and children. The #MeToo movement needs to ponder such blatant public efforts to saturate society with sexuality. We live in a time when mainstream newspapers can't be left open on the kitchen table for young eyes, as they are filled with embarrassingly raw language and discussions and depictions of sex, and the fawning promotion of what Augustine deplored as the "sin of Sodom."

Augustine struggled against his own sensual suffocation while in search of a higher truth. His resolution was to argue that if there was a God, then He himself must be the highest, most perfect love, downward from which other forms of love flowed, to the basest loves of our most beastly and binding appetites. Therefore, it's imperative for us not only to distinguish and rank the forms of love, but to actively repudiate the worst and seek the best: to discriminate.

Thus, having freed himself from the fetters of mere passion, Augustine helped shape the moral hierarchies of the Western world, thereby freeing it to pursue — or not — a higher ground in morality, law-making, the arts and sciences, and so much more. But we live in a world now busily repudiating his lesson in the name of egalitarian pluralism and diversity, a postmodern world that says there is nothing higher. Everything is a personal narrative constructed by hegemonic will, and there are no facts, only interpretations (Nietzsche). So back into the chains we go.

Having solved the question of what is good, Augustine then agonized over how it is possible to have a good God and a bad world. For 10 years, he argued — mistakenly, he came to say — that both good and evil were substances, like things, or forces, and just as his own spirit struggled with his flesh, the good and evil that God allowed on Earth are locked in perpetual struggle.

He freed himself from this idea when he further reasoned that if God was good, his whole cosmos must be good. Therefore, evil is not a thing, or a force. It arises from the absence of the good. This conclusion, too, has shaped our moral life and our whole body of law, because it conceives of humans as moral agents, capable of good or evil by use of our will in pursuit of good.

If we repudiate the good, evil will fill the vacuum. But this legacy has been corrupted. In modern Western society, our schools and courts are more likely to teach us that all bad behavior is a result of low income, or socialization, or abuse of some kind; that crime is not our fault, but the fault of our environment. We are back to the notion that evil springs from things.

Augustine's last struggle in "Confessions," like that of any youth straining to understand the stars, was with the existence of the cosmos itself. He undertakes an acute analysis of the nature of time as a response to the ancient question: If God made the universe, what existed before what we call the Big Bang?"

His answer is that time is simply a function of how we measure the relative movements and positions of things, such as planets and people. The world rotates once, we call it a day. One orbit of the sun, we call a year. But in itself, time doesn't exist. It is not a thing. Because the future is only what is not yet, and the past is only what has been, but is no longer. There is only the ongoing present: eternity. Just what was here when the universe in time was created. That was, and still is, an extraordinary notion.

Our way of undertaking the same interrogation was to send the $5 billion Hubble telescope into space to peer into the infinite, only to hear the late Stephen Hawking, the most fashionable cosmologist of recent times, concluding rather surprisingly — on behalf of the secular science of physics — that to know the answers to these questions will be "to know the mind of God." •

Edmund Burke was a British and Irish statesman, economist, and philosopher and member of parliament between 1766–1794 in the House of Commons of Great Britain with the Whig Party.

Source: Wikimedia Commons, public domain.

20. The Weakness of Libertarianism

DECEMBER 12, 2018

LIBERTARIANISM commands respect today as the only personal and political philosophy of the Western world standing in defense of individual freedom from state power. For that reason alone, it must be nourished. It is the last surviving remnant of old-style "classical liberalism," which began in 17th-century Europe as a philosophy poised against the absolute rulers of the age.

This early liberalism turned its guns on the power of the state and became the most important anti-statist, anti-centralization intellectual force of the Western world. In large measure, we can thank it for the constitutional safeguards against overbearing central power that were implanted in the American and Canadian constitutions.

This is to little avail today, as the courts in both nations have found ways to circumvent many of those safeguards.

The Evolution of Classical Liberalism

But this original and very successful classical liberalism movement eventually became disappointed with the actual results of liberty, with the bald fact that so many of the newly-free ended up poor and uneducated. So, it was slowly overtaken as well as co-opted by socialist radicals demanding state-funded social security and other benefits as a "higher freedom" for all. Today, modern liberalism has become our chief pro-statist political philosophy.

In other words, classical liberalism surrendered its original foundation in liberty and switched it up for a new foundation in forced equality. Society in general started to prefer more socialist and statist platforms.

Liberalism mutated from its original foundation in an equal start-line philosophy to an equal finish-line philosophy — from an anti-statist to a pro-statist party.

This has left us with modern libertarianism as the only clear defender of individual liberty, and in fulfilling this important task it has produced many of our most stirring protests against state power. However, sadly, libertarians often fail to recognize the weakness of their own otherwise very appealing philosophy: its doctrinaire disregard for any commonly shared conception of the good of society at which we ought to aim, not only as individuals but as a people.

This weakness exists because libertarians imagine there are only two players in the political game — the coercive state at the top and free individuals at the bottom. Political reality is far more complicated. In all free nations — distinctly not so in unfree ones — there are three players, not just two, and they are distinguished by their very different modes of control.

The state at the top has a monopoly on force, and its mode of control is power. This layer is the focus of centralizing socialists. At the bottom, there are free individuals whose signal mode of control is self-control. This layer is the focus of libertarians.

'Hands Off'

Between these two, in the middle layer, lies the only historically reliable protection from total state power that has ever been successful: a free and functioning civil society that is able to say to the state in the name of all: "Hands off!" Such resistance is only possible because, contrary to what libertarians believe, society is not "an abstraction" or "a fiction." It is far more than the sum of its individuals, and we know this because social and moral relationships cannot be derived from individuals alone.

That is why this is the layer that is the focus of true conservatives, as distinct from today's typical liberalized conservative. That is why a true conservative will speak, as did Edmund Burke, and David Hume before him, of the priority of "social freedom" over mere "individual freedom."

In order to achieve its considerable binding power, civil society must rely on social and moral authority, rather than on coercion or power. Just so, we freely and naturally accept the authority of our parents, coaches, teachers, and leaders (or reject it) to our benefit or at our peril. The control we feel among our fellow humans in civil society is indeed moral and social control, direction, inspiration, and yes, often prohibition and shame. It is the sum of all the acknowledged shalls and shall-nots of a free society.

What libertarians do not understand is the responsibility we all must share for the vigor or weakness of this middle layer, for they simply have nothing to say about this except, "Don't harm me." In other words, they have nothing to say about the many activities, policies, and beliefs that — beyond their destructive effect on mere individuals — may as clearly be destructive of civil society itself, of our traditions, customs, community standards, social affections, and the traditional decencies of our commonly held way of life. Indeed, if they do speak of such things, it is usually to protest that these, too, are forms of moral oppression, rather than our best defenses against state power.

It is in overlooking these fundamental truths and distinctions that we can fairly describe libertarianism as "a simple faith."

Its devotees miss the plain fact that it is value-sharing citizens concerned for far more than themselves as mere individuals who are the very best barrier against naked power. This is only possible when we behave as conscious participants in the creation of common moral bonds that make the good society something far more than the sum of its individual parts.•

Dirt jump — I will take control ...

Source: Wikimedia Commons, contributor Fischer.H

21. The Will to Control, the Will to Obey, and the Will to Be Free

NOVEMBER 26, 2018

IN a previous article, I described six kinds of freedom. And all my life, I have believed that in a democracy, freedom is the dominant passion of the people. But now I think not.

It is perhaps more correct to say that in modern times, at least, what we observe is a kind of shifting interplay, or a three-way struggle, between different aspects of Will. I think of these as the Will to Control, the Will to Obey, and the Will to be Free. These may be variously manifested in ourselves, in our relations with others, and in the political lives of nations.

Control

The Will to Control is the most obvious. It is expressed powerfully by most of us very early in life. The hysterical, out-of-control child who is actually seeking control of a parent or sibling in order to satisfy a want is the paradigm: hysteria as a form of control.

In the adult, the Will to Control is often the flip side of the Will to be Free, in that none is freer than he who can control his own circumstances and laws. In this last sentence lies the enduring theme and contradiction of all modern democratic theories, however, because obeying a law you make for yourself cannot be called obedience. It is more like a fulfillment of personal ambition.

Indeed, the deepest paradox of modern democratic theory is the idea that we can set up systems for controlling and obeying only our own laws, so that we can be free from others' control.

This belief persists, despite the fact that many non-democratic regimes have existed throughout history in which citizens were far more free than we are today. For starters, citizens (though not their slaves, who were noncitizens) were freer (less regulated and taxed) under ancient Athenian democracy than citizens of our modern democracies.

Many historians consider the citizens of ancient Rome, especially under the first post-democratic Roman Empire of Caesar Augustus (died A.D. 14), to have been the freest of all.

Those who lived under the British-based modern democracies — such as the United States and Canada — from the mid-1800s to about the middle of the 20th century were also more "free" than we are now. Although they had fewer listed (or newly invented) paper "rights" to brag about, they had more inherited traditional and actionable rights that were assumed by all and protected by powerful custom and common-law precedent.

They also suffered far less taxation and suffocating regulations than we do. Just over a hundred years ago, even the smell of an income tax — or any other tax on labor — was sufficient for citizens to march in the streets crying that they were about to become miserable "tax slaves," for a tax on goods and imports was considered acceptable, while a tax on labor was considered deeply immoral. But we are all tax slaves now.

In ordinary life, the Will to Control is most visible in the storied career climb to the top, and the general drive for financial success. In politics, it's embodied in the party organizer and, above all, in the schemer (most politicians in democracies, who must rely on popularity at all costs) who is always ready to manipulate others as a means to some cherished political ambition.

In realpolitik, control-hysteria finds its ultimate expression in pogroms, liquidations, genocides, tortures, and concentration camps. The historical prototype is the tyrant, and — most dangerous of all — the beloved modern dictator, described with such fawning terms as "Redeemer," "Fuhrer," or "Duce," because he has archly — and usually democratically — discovered in the masses a latent Will to Obey.

On that score, we tend to invoke apathy as an excuse for such fawning obedience, as if the apathetic have no will. But on the contrary, apathy is among the strongest expressions of an active Will to Obey in all who deeply yearn to surrender the burdens and responsibilities of control — and especially in those who wish to escape the responsibilities entailed by their own freedom.

Obedience

In ordinary life, we see this obedience-relief at work in the misbehaving child who in truth is yearning for guidance and so eventually submits to real authority; in the employee who happily performs slavish, even demeaning work in exchange for a mediocre salary and the guarantee of ample benefits; and generally, in all those who seek the peace of security and the avoidance of risk — which is to say, most people.

No one understands this better than the harried control freak who comes to heel the moment he encounters a superior power. He is the type who is — as Churchill put it when describing the authoritarian personality of the Hun — "either at your throat, or at your feet."

Politically, the Will to Obey is visible in the stunning apathy of the masses, notoriously and dramatically so in the ease with which one camp guard with a cheap pistol can control thousands. Less dramatically, but oh, so prevalently, is the willingness of the masses everywhere to surrender so much in the way of their basic freedoms for welfare, health care, government pensions, and countless regulations and programs designed to control myriad aspects of their daily lives.

In the wake of failing religious belief and moral authority, people look to such redemptive political regimes because they promise a progressive secular salvation. This promise is easily met by leaders who understand the intimate relationship between the Will to Control and the Will to Obey.

Freedom

The pure Will to be Free is another matter. Though we imagine it the strongest and most noble aspect of Will — and this is certainly true for the very few truly noble people — it is for most the weakest form of Will, trumped everywhere by the desire for control and obedience.

By any fair estimate, only about a quarter of human beings on the planet today enjoy anything close to a "free" society (and, as mentioned, even our "free" democracies are objectively far less free than were the same societies in quite recent times).

Even though we all have tasted the delights of personal freedom, it is usually experienced physically, as a personal indulgence to do or to have whatever we want, however briefly. Or we have experienced it as one of those sweet moments that come after some keen but long-denied satisfaction has finally stilled the yearning soul.

It is no accident that today, when the claims of the body and its appetites trump spiritual concerns, our contemporary clamoring for freedom comes down to a kind of endless striving, not for true freedom and its burden, but for "rights" to sexual pleasures, to abortion, to euthanasia, to "free" medical care, to welfare benefits, and so on — all of which have to do with the wants of, or fears for, our own bodies, but have little to do with the body politic.

Although modern democratic systems begin with the Will to be Free, they can quickly transform into regimes more concerned with Control (by the few) and Obedience (by the rest).

The astute German-Italian sociologist Robert Michels famously argued that all democracies obey an "iron law of oligarchy," and they all inevitably end as such.

And I have argued in a previous article that the pattern for all Western democracies is something that ought to be called libertarian-socialism, in which the most cherished freedoms are purely individual and private (and to repeat, concern mostly sex and our bodies), while states take up the responsibilities of the broader aspects of our lives (in the form of multilayered government services, benefits, and guarantees for which we "free" citizens are very heavily taxed).

This is so true that the ostensibly free citizen, who in many nations now pays half of his income in taxes of all kinds, in effect works half of every year for the state.

Looking only at the recent history of the moral and intellectual contortions required to justify our underlying ideal of freedom — of control of the free masses by themselves — we may conclude, especially in view of the number of responsibilities and real freedoms we have either spurned or surrendered to the state, that this ideal stands as somewhat of a monument to human cleverness and self-deception.•

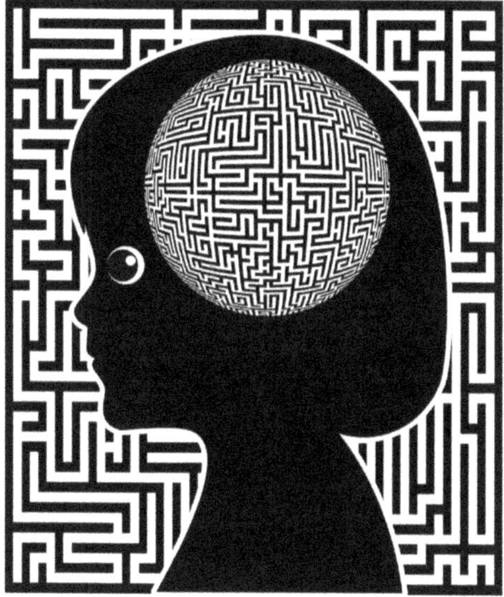

Young male and female brains work in different ways.

Source: Shutterstock, 388276666, Sangoiri.

22. To Deny Sex Differences Is to Harm Society

NOVEMBER 5, 2018 (UPDATED: MARCH 2, 2019)

PLATO sowed the wind of sexual egalitarianism a long time ago. So did Karl Marx, his sugar-daddy Friedrich Engels, and Leo Tolstoy.

Then came the kibbutz system of Israel. Then, the radically anti-male, anti-marriage, and anti-family feminists of the West, who jumped on that bandwagon in the mid-20th century.

Now, we're reaping the whirlwind.

George Gilder sounded the alarm in his prescient 1992 book "Men and Marriage," with a warning that is quite telling, given today's bitter war between the sexes. To wit, the prevalent sexual instinct of males the world over — to the great detriment of social stability — is to focus on their immediate gratification. Single, young men, undisciplined and unconstrained by traditional sexual mores and manners, are a distinct hazard to society and its procreative health, for many reasons.

Among the reasons: They vastly prefer hit-and-run sex. They are wildly more physically and sexually aggressive than females. Although young, single men represent a low percentage of the population over the age of 14, they commit the majority of violent crimes. They drink more and have more serious car accidents than women or married men. Young bachelors are 22 times more likely to be committed for mental problems — and 10 times more likely to be hospitalized for chronic diseases than married men. Single men also are convicted of rape five times more often than married men, and have almost double the mortality rate of married men — and three times that of single women.

Losing Out

The whole business of sexual liberation has backfired. Men have benefited sexually in the short term, but not necessarily in the long haul. Women have lost in both because they have surrendered the one sure means — the postponement of immediate male gratification — that enabled them to have children, provide for them, protect them, and nurture them personally at the same time.

In essence, the traditional balancing equation that drew men into the powerfully attractive fertility world of the female has been surrendered and, instead, we have encouraged females to enter the frenetically sexual world of men.

A direct result has been the weakening of marriage and family bonds; men abandoning women and children; and many — mostly poor women and their children — abandoning marriage altogether and cleaving unto the patriarchal state.

Even worse, as Gilder explains, feminism, by default, has allowed males to create an informal system of serial (or even simultaneous) polygamy — one in which the stronger (wealthier, more successful) men can enjoy many, usually younger, partners. But a woman loses out, in that, for the purposes of child-bearing, her chances of locating a strong husband and father for her children are biologically confined to a few fleeting years of her life. If she waits too long to marry, the strong males her own age get taken in a rapidly peaking, concave-sided pyramid of diminishing choices.

Furthermore, in societies that choose to deny these natural sex differences and to permit "liberated" sex, the homosexual sub-culture vies for normalcy with the core culture, attacks traditional values, and recruits otherwise procreative (and usually younger) males. And because liberation so obviously multiplies the sexual choices for strong males, it overturns the equal apportionment of possible mates, and, in its feminist guise, sets the female ethos against the male ethos, thereby encouraging sexual resentment between men and women.

In April, Alek Minassian took his rented van on a mile-long death-ride along a Toronto sidewalk, killing 10 people and injuring 13 others. His motive? He claimed allegiance to a male grievance group called "incel," which stands for "involuntarily celibate." He and his group were violently angry about unequal apportionment. The victims he mowed down were mostly women.

Death of Marriage

All of this leads to fewer marriages, something we saw first in Sweden halfway through the last century, when it enthusiastically embraced sexual liberation: Its marriage rate did a freefall to around 50 percent of its former level.

And then, more people began living alone. Today, almost 60 percent of the residents of Stockholm live alone — a growing pattern seen everywhere in the West. For downtown Seattle, that number is now over 70 percent.

Meanwhile, easy divorce — or "couple dissolution" as the Swedes so coyly call it — has risen drastically everywhere. Multiple mates? Easy sex? Homosexuality? Easy cohabitation and divorce? All these inevitably undermine heterosexual monogamy, which is most unfortunate, precisely because "monogamy is designed to minimize the effect of sexual inequalities — to prevent the powerful of either sex from disrupting the familial order," Gilder says.

And so, as Gilder warns, because the most crucial process of civilization is "the subordination of male sexual impulses and biology to the long-term horizons of female sexuality," society must be set up to tame men and their barbaric proclivities. For without the long-range reproductive goals of women, men would be content to fight, enjoy their lust, wander, make war, compete, and strive for power, glory, and dominance.

The conclusion is that, in terms of the larger purposes, and indeed the very survival of human civilization — which depends utterly on sufficient procreation, successful child-nurturing, and strong families — males, in general, are inferior sexually to women, who, because of their biology, control the entirety of the sexual and procreative order (or disorder) of human life.

In this sense only, males are neither sexually nor morally equal to females, and therefore — and this is surely Gilder's most important point — "men must be made equal by society." Which is to say that men rely for personal meaning and success on the socially purposive roles created for them by their culture.

In short, women channel and confine the generalized male sexual desire in such a way as to protect themselves and their children, and in so doing, they teach men to subordinate their impulses to the long-term cycles of female sexuality and biology on which civilization, and its survival, has always depended.

When you stop to deeply consider the complex physical, emotional, and financial requirements of the average family, the seriousness of this undertaking sinks in. It requires what the anthropologist Margaret Mead called a "commitment of permanence" from each sex, and a "deal" struck between the parties, the terms of which are supplied by the culture. We have been breaking the deal at our own — and especially at our children's — peril.•

Liberty Leading the People by Eugène Delacroix, 1830. Musée du Louvre, Paris.

Source: Wikimedia Commons, public domain.

23. Six Kinds of Freedom

Throughout history, there have been many different notions of freedom

I HAVE a reflex affection for the word "freedom." But what does it mean?

Most people answer: "It means doing what you want." This common response speaks for an age — our own — that equates freedom with personal satisfaction. But throughout history, there have been many different notions of freedom.

For the ancients, as mentioned in my previous article on the meaning of a Senate, it meant not being a slave. For the Christian, it has always meant living according to the precepts of Christ. For the Enlightenment thinker of the 18th century, it meant living according to Reason. For the Romantic, it meant the expression of authentic emotion.

It seems a multi-faceted, if not entirely muddled concept. So I have attempted a working classification of the different kinds of freedom. To my mind, there are at least six. But first, a loose distinction between freedom and liberty seems necessary, as these two words are often used interchangeably.

I think "liberty" should be used mostly to refer to freedom in its physical context. A man in jail, for example, has almost zero liberty, and if he escapes, we say he is "at liberty." But even when in jail, with no liberty, he has a lot of freedom in the sense that he can still choose among myriad options, attitudes, and values. He can sleep, count the miles while pacing the floor, or write poetry, lie to the warden to protect a fellow criminal, or tell the truth.

Most of us, it seems, use our freedom to restrict our own liberty in all sorts of ways. Mortgages, bank loans, contracts, leases, business deals, and family and personal promises and obligations are mostly how we use our freedom to restrict our liberty.

1. Internal Freedom

The most basic kind of freedom is internal to everyone, and can't be avoided even if we try, for we must then freely choose among attempts to avoid. Internal freedom is of the greatest personal intimacy and secretiveness. It's the hidden core of our being, is unknowable by others, distinguishes us from the animal kingdom, and from each other, and is the basis on which we are able to become moral — or amoral, or immoral — beings.

That is why some people call this moral freedom. But this kind of freedom is not, in itself, moral. It is the unique capacity we all have to become moral or immoral, according to how we use our internal freedom. Once, when teaching a class, a student said, "That's too secretive. I wish we all had, like a mini-TV screen on our foreheads, then we would all be more honest with each other."

"I don't think so," I replied. "I think we'd all be walking around with one hand over our foreheads."

2. Self-Freedom

It is a bit odd to say we should be free from our own selves. But, in fact, most of the world's freedom talk, at least as found in the great religions and philosophical movements, has had to do with this kind of freedom — in the sense of learning how to escape the seductions of our own passions and the pitfalls of ignorance. We can't be free if our emotions dictate what we will do.

But in our neo-romantic age, this idea has been turned upside down, and the expression of the authentic feelings of one's "true self" elevated to the superior position. Today, we even hear people pass off plain rudeness or off-color language as "authenticity." And we hear others declare, as if on a spiritual quest: "I am trying to find my true self" (although no one ever seems to ask how we would know whether the self-seeking or the self-sought, is the true self). They seek freedom from restraint. This inversion of the traditional relation of mind to feeling has produced what our forebears would have called a disorder of the soul.

3. External Freedom
("Freedom From")

External freedom refers to the normal and natural freedom of external action expected in daily life by most people throughout history (though seldom fully realized). It is sometimes described as freedom from, because it implies immunity from undue interference by others or by the state. It's also sometimes called "negative freedom," meaning the absence of constraints on living one's own life, and the right to do anything not forbidden by law (in contrast to totalitarian systems that mostly allow only what is permitted by law).

Many in the Western tradition consider this (in combination with political freedom, explained next), to be the most important concept of freedom, and liberal constitutionalism (now under attack in many places) has been its political expression in the West. We can think of this freedom as the "original position" of most human beings, prior to any consideration of the laws commanding or prohibiting their behavior.

4. Political Freedom
("Freedom To")

Political freedom has to do with establishing certain predictable and expressed rights of action to do this or that (whether we invoke them or not), along with specific limits to government power so that we can take charge of our own lives. The most common political freedoms, at least in the free world, are the right to speak freely, to associate with people of your choice, to own property, to worship, to leave and re-enter your country, to be tried by a jury of your peers, to vote in elections (if you live in a democracy), among others.

When we have sufficient freedom to do these things (though to speak truthfully, we are only free to do them if no one stops us), we think of them as the rights of a free society (which may or may not be a democratic one). For example, ancient Athens had most of these things, but wasn't democratic in our modern sense of the word, because at least a third of the citizens of Athens were slaves, and women had no vote. England had all these rights almost two centuries before she became fully democratic.

5. Collective, or "Higher" Freedom ("Freedom For")

Some commentators take the view that external freedom and political freedom are just formal concepts that mean very little to the poor and disadvantaged. Or that they are just a recipe for a chaotic liberal society, an uncivil nightmare of clashing wills and disconnected citizens. What is really needed, they argue, is a "higher freedom" based on a collective will to achieve a higher common good. This could be called "freedom for," because it is based on an ideology of collective unity that prescribes distinct social and moral values and objectives for all.

Under this ideal of freedom, the state is expected to control the production and supply of most basic citizen needs, thus giving them freedom-from-want. All totalitarian states openly, and all modern welfare states more covertly and messily, rest on this ideal of collective freedom and believe the classical-liberal idea of protecting individuals from their own government isn't logical if the government is the embodiment of their will in the first place.

6. Spiritual Freedom

In its purest form, this type of freedom comes from striving for a complete identification with God (or God's will, or perhaps with all creation) to arrive at a condition of soul that transcends the confusion and disharmony of the self, the body, and the entire material and political world. There are many types here, but at the extreme some seekers after this kind of spiritual freedom take starkly opposing routes.

They may engage in a kind of libertinism of the flesh, on the grounds that the body is of no importance whatsoever and so may be used, abused, and enjoyed until it is spent (ancient Gnostics and perpetually stoned hippie mystics come to mind). Or, they take the ascetic route and deny the flesh altogether, as do many religious leaders on the grounds that worldly needs and longings prevent the achievement of complete spiritual freedom.

This is an incomplete classification. But the next time someone asks a question about freedom, it may help to ask in return: "What kind of freedom do you mean?"•

The Chamber of the Senate of Canada.

Source: Wikimedia Commons, Saffron Blaze, public domain.

24. Abolish the Senate? Not so Fast!

OCTOBER 22, 2018

IN our long Western tradition, the changing conceptions of what a senate ought to be are intimately related to changing conceptions of human nature. They thus serve as a kind of mirror with which to see ourselves as we grapple with the most important political question: How should we make laws?

The senates of ancient Greece and Rome, despite their differences, shared an underlying classical model of human nature considered universally true: Human beings are willful and impulsive, and therefore prone to error in the measure that their actions are heated and hasty.

For the pagan, this was an eternal truth of human nature. For the Christian, human beings were once perfect in Eden, but fell into sin and error through disobedience to God.

Common to both pagan and Christian beliefs, however, was the commonsensical belief that will and emotion originate in the heart and appetitive parts of the body, whereas reason originates in reflection, in the head.

Accordingly, our standard picture of humanity has been of a divided being tormented by a lifelong internal struggle between will and reason, each vying to be master by making the other a slave.

This master/slave metaphor emerged naturally from slave societies, in which freedom was not defined as the ability to do whatever you might want as long as you don't harm someone else, but as not being a slave. The goal of all free people was to be a rational being who was master of his or her own passions.

Human Nature

As it was for the body, so it should be for the body politic. The architects of the ancient democracies felt that the public passions, like the private passions, should be acknowledged and heard, but never given control over the whole political body.

So, in the Greek democracy under Demosthenes, for example, a senate comprising older and more experienced citizens proposed the laws, and the people voted on them, yea or nay. But the law-making "initiative" was with the senate.

The laws came down from the senate to the people, rather than the other way around as in the modern democracies, in some of which even convicts are considered part of the people, and allowed to vote on the laws.

For the founders of America and Canada, the master/slave metaphor was accepted as an obvious fact of personal and political life: The people and their factions will tend to be emotional, willful, and prone to error and, in a simple majoritarian democracy, will always crush minorities.

Constitutions must be designed to block this tendency. Hence, an appointed Upper House or Senate equating to reason and filled with wiser and older people, who have a stake in the country but are untouched by politics, must have the right to frustrate, and even to block, the will of the people in a Lower House. To omit such a check on the impulsivity of the people is to render them slaves to their own passions.

In retrospect, however, it seems clear that the changing role of senates in the West (the American Senate became popularly elective in 1913, while the Canadian Senate is so far still appointive) is an institutional reflection of how human nature is (re)imagined at particular historical periods.

In conservative periods of high skepticism concerning natural human goodness, the safety check of an appointed Senate has always been called for to protect the people from themselves! Restraint is then the cry.

Conversely, in a modern liberal period when a belief in natural human goodness runs high, we hear loud cries for more direct democracy, to change appointive Senates to elective, and even for the abolition of senates entirely, because they are widely viewed as an intolerable brake on the pure (and purely good) will of the People. Freedom is then the cry.

The core question is whether or not unchecked human will is good by nature. Modern liberals will tend to say yes, and conservatives, no.

Popular Will

Ever since the Romantic sentiments that arose in the late 18th century when thinkers — and poets such as Wordsworth, Shelley, and Whitman — first began so forcefully to insist on natural human goodness, and hence to argue that we are corrupted not by ourselves but by imperfect laws and institutions, the trend of the Western democracies has been to argue that human nature, passions, and appetites must be less restrained.

This is clearly visible today in our widespread release of legal and moral restraints on sex, divorce, homosexuality, pornography, abortion, euthanasia, drugs, natural gender distinctions, and much else.

In 2013, a former leader of Canada's Parliamentary Opposition published an open letter to Canada's senators in the National Post in which he opined that "the greatest weakness of our appointed Senate as presently constituted is that Senators are unelected and unaccountable to electors. The Senate lacks the democratic legitimacy required to command public support."

If we accept the liberal belief that the will of the people is usually and inevitably good, then he is right on, as they say. But if we accept the conservative view that the unalloyed will of the people ought to be restrained and improved by independent "sober second thought" — that reason (a senate) must always stand ready to correct will (a Commons, or House of Representatives), and not the other way around, then such a view is quite wrong-headed.

It all boils down to the acceptance or rejection of the master/slave metaphor of human nature.

The weakness of the recurring liberal effort to dissolve the metaphor — by conflating will with reason — is obvious and visible in the political gridlock that manifests when two elective bodies each claim democratic legitimacy.

The weakness of the conservative case is the paucity of senators of sufficiently high character and independent mind who refuse in principle to self-corrupt or to become slaves of popular will.

This is the mirror in which we are reflected.•

Totalitarian leaders Joseph Stalin, Adolf Hitler, Mao Zedong, Benito Mussolini, and Kim Il-sung.

Source: Wikimedia Commons, public domain.

25. 'Libertarian–Socialism': How Modern Democracy Overcame Its Own Contradiction

OCTOBER 14, 2018

THE totalitarian states of the 20th century, whether of national socialist (Nazi and fascist) or international socialist (communist) ambitions, were aiming to control and organize almost every aspect of life from the top down: to bring about by force of law and government what is broadly described as "the triumph of the Will over Nature."

The Germans called this process *Gleichschaltung*, or "bringing into line." They tried to organize by force the naturally different lives of millions of private citizens, according to a single totalizing vision of the good society.

A great irony of the political history of the West that surprises most people is that all of these totalitarian systems, as the late political philosopher Michael Oakeshott put it, are "the ungracious children" of democracy. All dictators have waited breathlessly for the roar of the crowd, just as modern democratic leaders wait for the roar of the polls.

In the deepest sense, then, the World War II confrontation between the "free world" and its children — the totalitarian political systems — was, and remains, a confrontation of the West with itself.

In the end, those defiantly totalizing systems were largely defeated in the European theater (though they simmer still — the current bastion of communism in the West is located in our universities).

But this left all liberal-democratic regimes (themselves already launched on a disturbingly similar, if slower and softer, path to state-guaranteed perfection) faced with a common ultimate question: "How are we to equalize, subsidize, control, and guarantee by force of law (by the will of the democratic state), more equal conditions of life for all (as those totalitarian states were trying to do), and still call ourselves free?"

In short, how are we to overcome the ideological contradiction that arises from trying to build a polity on a foundation of liberty and forced equality at the same time?

"Divide and conquer" would be the answer.

Freedom and Control

The first step was the conceptual division of the body politic into two bodies: a private body and a public body, each with its own justifying ideology.

There would be unprecedented freedom of individual will for all things personal and private — especially those having to do with sex and the body, such as abortion rights, easy divorce, homosexual rights, contraception rights, transgender rights, saturation pornography, gay marriage, euthanasia rights, and so on — all legally abetted, and in many democracies subsidized, or free of charge, giving the subliminal message that "We, the People" have never been so free.

But at the same time, in most once minimally regulated democracies, and with astonishing speed, there would be the aggressive exercise of a pervasive public will — a new and vast public realm funded by massively increased taxation and permanent public debt, extending the tentacles of state control into a myriad of private lives, properties, social, artistic, and athletic activities, and commercial operations, while positioning the state as the generous benefactor, regulator, and protector of all, equally.

The result is that the typical citizen of a modern democracy now lives, in all private matters, like the ideal libertarian, who demands complete individual freedom with respect to all things private, personal, sexual, and moral that he or she can imagine and defend as compliant while not harming others.

But with respect to all things public, the citizen is living like the socialist, who reaches reflexively for government solutions and support of as many social and economic goods and services as the state has deemed it feasible to provide.

"What is the government going to do about this?" is today the most common question from citizens.

The Unspoken Trade

The result is that although historically libertarians and socialists have always despised each other's ideologies — each was developed specifically to oppose the other — the two have been successfully fused, beyond the dreams of even the most ambitious social planner, into a hybrid system. This synthesis, while perfectly neither, is part-libertarian and part-socialist, with a visible dividing barrier between the two domains, the simple physical counterpart of which is … your skin.

The end result is our novel regime type: a fusion of opposites that has become pervasive in the Western world in an astonishingly short period of time.

To achieve it, the unspoken trade offered as a lure was the understanding that the people wouldn't bemoan their diminished real political, property, and economic freedoms, and the permeation of their lives by high taxation and minutely invasive regulation, if they were allowed more sexual and bodily freedoms in exchange.

This Faustian deal has been offered to "the people" by all democratic states to escape their own ideological contradiction: Give me control over your broader citizen liberties, and I will give you all the private rights and pleasures of the body.

Libertarian–socialism is now a homogenized regime-type throughout the West. This new trans-ethnic, trans-national form as ubiquitous as Coca-Cola and the cell phone has, by way of erotic seduction (the private pleasures and freedoms of the body) and a policy trade-off (an equality of public goods and services effected by way of a bountiful tax harvest), been so conducive to the growth of bureaucratic statism that almost all the modern democracies have already become what I call "tripartite states."

These are states in which one-third of the people work to create wealth, one-third (when we include all full-time and part-time employees, and permanent government contracts) are employed by government at some level, and one-third receive significant annual income or benefits in kind from the state.

Once this final stage of the democratic mutation is reached there can be no return, except through eventual catastrophic decline, for in the voting booth, the last two segments will naturally and always gang up on the first, like two wolves and a sheep voting on what to have for dinner!•

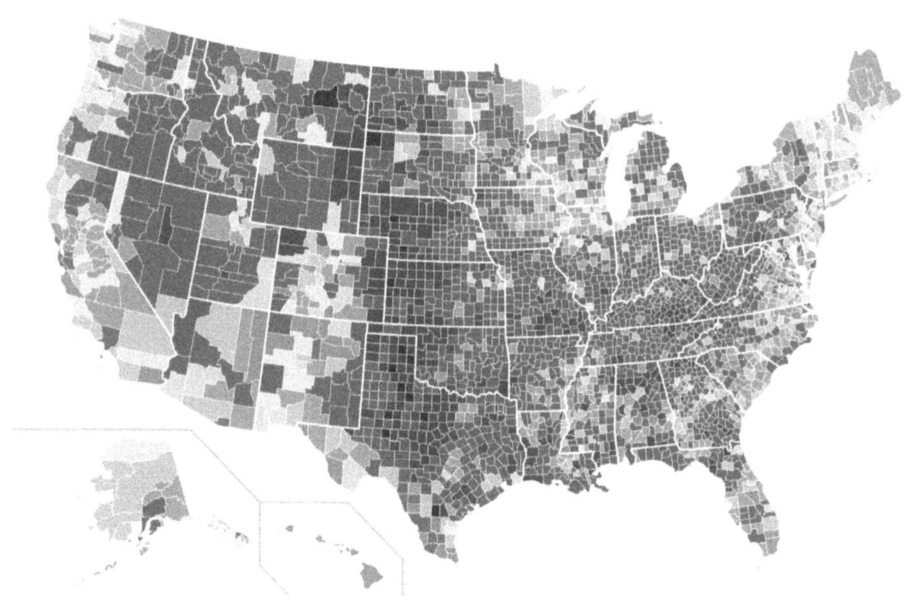

United States presidential election results by county, November 8, 2016.

Source: Wikipedia, public domain.

26. The Split Personality of the 'Anti-Polis'

OCTOBER 14, 2018

The urban/rural divide is at the heart of the political divide

THIS familiar map of the 2016 American election, broken down by black (representing Republican) and white (representing Democrat) counties — rather than by states — shows a stark division of citizens in a rural/urban pattern that has become typical of most Western democracies.

Much about urbanization is explained by the attraction of better jobs, services and the glitter of wealth. However, there is another powerful, less visible attraction. Namely, the fact that life in the "big city" provides immediate access to a hedonistic privacy, offering relief from the traditional moral restraints and obligations imposed by civil life in rural settings.

The Rural/Urban Divide

The rural/urban divide became especially visible in America over the previous election cycle, and an *Atlantic Monthly* article from 2012, "Red State, Blue City: How the Urban-Rural Divide is Splitting America," remarked that "virtually every major city (100,000 plus population) in the United States of America has a different outlook from the less populous areas that are closest to it. The difference is no longer where people live, it's about how people live."

The pattern of big cities dissolving their own moral roots is an old one, and literature is often the canary in the coal mine warning of dark and rapacious cities where almighty money, unbridled self-interest and sensuality chip away at ordinary morality.

French writer Gustave Flaubert's newly citified "Madame Bovary" grinds down to suicide after losing herself in vanity and infidelity. Charles Dickens's "The Life and Adventures of Martin Chuzzlewit" brutally exposes the cash-cruelty of American city life under its new aristocracy of money. And who could forget Thomas Hardy's lovely, dark-tressed "Tess of the d'Urbervilles" milking her cows at Talbothays dairy farm, the soulless urban sprawl of Flintcomb-Ash encroaching to swallow her up?

One of the most disturbing literary characterizations of a growing modern anomie — that condition, first described minutely by French sociologist Emile Durkheim in which society ceases to provide any moral guidance for individuals — is sensed with some alarm in the first line of Albert Camus's "The Stranger."

Meursault, the title character, opens the novel with these listless words: "Mama died today. Or, maybe yesterday; I don't know." He doesn't know because the bonds are broken, and in a war-torn, morally wracked Europe, of which he is so often taken as a symbol, so is he.

The greatest painter of deracinated souls, however, was surely Russian novelist Fyodor Mikhailovich Dostoevsky.

For Dostoevsky, who first captured the irony that in the modern city, rootlessness is the most-common bond, and if it is true that God doesn't exist, then "everything is permitted."

When everything is permitted, there can be no possible distinction between good and evil, and, therefore, no ordering principles by which a society can form a "cosmion" — a term used by some philosophers to describe a sheltering common life in which precisely by way of such distinctions citizens voluntarily modify their personal choices for the good of all, rather than primarily for their own good. The thought that by virtue of an enfeebling mutation of this grounding possibility the Western world may be morally imploding, all the while defending the outcome as the highest form of democratic liberty, is rather disquieting.

Hyper-Democracies

For just as molecules may break into atoms and corporate bodies into mere aggregates, a democracy can fragment into a "hyper-democracy" — a simple arithmetical compilation of sovereign individuals, each cheerfully self-alienated from any search for a common good and therefore from each other.

The result is mass anomie: an aimless collection of citizens it is assumed will determine the blind outcome of society. This is a type of political formlessness that can arise only from the privatization of liberty, and it differs sharply from the classical democratic form — under assault, but still with us as late as mid-20th century — which was a system striving for an ostensible common good, the underlying, if unspoken logic of which was that human acts directed exclusively toward ourselves as individuals can have no moral substance.

They acquire this only when directed toward others, which is to say, when they are self-transcendent acts that bond all citizens in a civil society through mutual obligations and duties.

It goes without saying that such a society can't be a fiction, as libertarians are prone to believe, for it has a relational moral being that is necessarily greater than the sum of its parts.

However imperfect, that was the notion that energized the ancient city, or polis, the principal aim of which was to thrive as a unified social, moral, and — if barbarians were at the gate — a military entity.

However, modern democracies have turned this notion on its head, by allowing a new, soft sort of urban barbarism to develop inside their own gates. For over the past century, each at its own pace, they have been mutating from polis to anti-polis, to aggregates of sometimes millions of urbanites living side-by-side (hard to say "together"), offering an easy evasion of the moral expectations of others, and a shared, often deliberate and outspoken repudiation of any felt obligation to create such expectations for others.

Anti-Community Communities

So, now, and uniquely so in human history, we have gigantic anti-community communities producing anti-morality moralities, so to speak. That millions of citizens wander past each other staring in voluntary isolation at their cell phones, is just a recent high-tech manifestation of this long-developing truth for which they were already primed. It's not as if human communities, as corporate bodies, have never decayed into amoral aggregates before.

Ancient Rome remains a classic case. Our modern hyper-democratic regimes may be the first in history intentionally and defiantly to engineer this kind of moral implosion by philosophical fiat.

Why "philosophical"? Because what is so clearly demarcated on our map looks very much like a pattern formed by citizens who over a century-and-a-half have taken sides in the long philosophical, political and moral contest between the incompatible social philosophies of J.S. Mill and Edmund Burke, which is to say, as *The Atlantic* article above warned, how we ought to live.

However dumbed-down, Mill's so-called "Do whatever you want as long as you don't harm someone else" rules the cities, while Burke's notion of civil society as a polity voluntarily bonded by "little platoons" still rules the rural areas.

I am sure he was speaking of cities when a historian colleague wrote, "the modern world seeks absolute autonomy, freedom of choice unbounded by norms. We do not wish to obey moral laws, but to create them for ourselves."

It's mostly in our fashionable cities that we see this trend, while country folk, even when they use the same democratic language, still so far intend the basic principle of our original, if now decaying, style of a polis democracy.

An ironic result of the conflation of a corporate civil body and a mere aggregate of individuals is that the word — indeed, the very concept of "democracy" — has bifurcated and is now something that will do whatever is asked of it, such that it isn't uncommon to hear two people in the same room cite democracy to defend plainly incompatible moral and philosophical positions, as if merely to utter the word with sufficient solemnity is to rescue a bad argument.

This has utterly stranded any underlying notion of "the people."

They have become like a pack of dogs which, though each is still tethered to the carriage of public life by virtue of the right to vote, otherwise have no traces to join them to each other, and so will run at will in all directions with no common destination.

Where the carriage will end up is anybody's guess, and the sobering possibility looms that no one cares. The hyper-democratic ship — to alter the metaphor — must have no chart, no captain, no pilot — just equally liberated passengers. Liberated from each other, that is, each citizen increasingly his or her own private morals-inventing machine. Census analysts in many parts of the West continue to warn of the high and climbing percentages of urban residents — ranging from 50 to 75 percent in some cities — who now live alone.

Accordingly, the modern anti-polis is increasingly a place where acts traditionally considered wrong, or "bad for society," which is to say, bad for the good of the polis, such as divorce, abortion, single-parenting, homosexuality, drug-use, and saturation pornography, increase in variety and number and are normalized by language-inversion, and then defended vigorously against "judgmental" attacks — on what?

Not on these behaviors themselves, or on any harm to society as a whole, these acts may cause now, or in future, but on the sanctity of the individual right to choose them. For what could possibly shame a polity with vanishingly few shared convictions? Not much.

As a result, the anti-polis has become the locus of a cultural-moral relativism easily identifiable in such angry prohibitions as: "Don't you dare judge me!"

The red hinterland, meanwhile, remains rooted, however tenuously, in our original and natural biological model for a human community and continues to rail privately, if not freely — except in the ballot box — against these and many other once publicly recognized wrongs.

Social and Moral Debilitation Visible in Cities

The evidence for what looks very much like social and moral self-debilitation is for now mostly visible in cities, where increasingly, we find the most extreme statistics on every imaginable human predilection, perversity, and indulgence, and a dire breakdown of the natural family (best defined as "a married mother and father living together with their dependent children") unequaled since the last stages of Roman decadence.

This is paralleled by a growing dependency of broken families on government. Isn't it shocking to realize that even the combined disaster of two exhausting and bloody World Wars book-ending a devastating international depression couldn't produce the depths of social, family, and moral breakdown now observable in the crime, health, and welfare statistics of most big cities? It's hard to resist the old quip that these may be the only entities in history to have passed from barbarism to decadence without passing through civilization.

I don't want to exaggerate.

The modern city is a living paradox. Wonderful art collections are on display in architecturally impressive buildings, on the steps of which, bums may be seen sleeping off their drug of choice or begging.

Urban advance and decline may grow together, even feed off each other in reaction, the former masking the latter. Great museums, orchestras, and art shows glow like ever more carefully-applied make-up on the worried visage of the anti-polis, which still harbors many small tightly bonded communities: households, churches, charities, and institutions clinging, beleaguered, to their private vision of a shared common good.

Many of these are immigrant or remnant communities clustering against what they see as an obvious decline of the surrounding society, bombarded daily by newly-legitimized — if not approved — behaviors that in the very recent past (in a now-defunct phrase) would have "shamed us all."

Finally, our modern anti-polis entities have become repositories for most of the rich, as well as most of the poor of democratic nations. The preponderance of benefits goes in one direction, with those in the middle gradually driven out by higher prices, by a simple evaporation of their former standard of living, or by self-relocation to cheaper suburbs as a service class. Hence the split-personality of the anti-polis.

The well-off frequent theater and symphony subsidized by governments and corporations travel abroad, hire the best lawyers, eat in very nice restaurants, and drive their kids, or have Filipina nannies walk them to the best schools.

While those at the other extreme can't escape bad, even dangerous schools, have latchkey kids, the greatest share of fatherless children and abortions, get arrested for most of the alcohol, drug use, and domestic violence — and are generally struggling in the underbelly of the anti-polis.

During the long decline of Rome, if they escaped assassination, wealthy citizens bypassed a similar reality — while sampling similar amusements — by retreating to their country villas, just as wealthy moderns retreat by clustering in pricey neighborhoods or gated suburban communities, riding it all down in style.

Skeptical citizens in the countryside, meanwhile, continue to resist what looks to them "like an alien invasion" of the nation by city-dwellers, as Walter Lippmann put it back in 1927 — the first year America had more urban than rural citizens. The aliens sniff that citizens in the red counties are "living in the 19th century," while the latter are convinced beyond all reasonable doubt that those in the blue counties inhabit a weird — and possibly sick — world celebrating the hegemony of individual will over all other moral claims, even over the primacy of human nature.

The latest weirdness on public display is the right of individuals to repudiate their own natural biology by re-imagining themselves as any gender, or combination of genders they wish, and hence of men to enter women's washrooms at will, and vice versa.

Aliens, indeed! Red counties vote against blue because the anti-polis is offensive to everything they have ever believed.•

www.ingramcontent.com/pod-product-compliance
Lightning Source LLC
Chambersburg PA
CBHW050000040726
47599CB00014B/1145